Vedic Value System

A Key to Modern World Crisis

Edited and Compiled

by

Dr. Ravi Prakash Arya

AMAZON BOOKS, USA

In Association with

INDIAN FOUNDATION FOR VEDIC SCIENCE

H.O.1051, Sector-1, Rohtak, Haryana, India Ph. 01262-292580

Delhi Contact Ph. Nos.: 09313033917; 09650183260

Emails: vedicscience@rediffmail.com; vedicscience@hotmail.com

Website: www.vedascience.net

First Edition

Kali era: 5117 (c. 2015)
Kalpa era: 1,97,29,49,117
Brahma era: 15,50,21,97,9,49,117

ISBN No. 81-87710-94-2

Contents

Preface

Today we are living in a world of crisis, in spite of the so-called advancement of science and technology. The scientific advancement and development of high technology might have blessed humanity with some material comforts. Nevertheless, it has cursed humanity at large with poverty, hunger, disturbances, terrorism, environmental and cultural pollutions everywhere. All this scientific advancement has added to our miseries and problems. Why? The answer is there is a blind race for artha (material gains) through science and technology, but the major factor of dharma (value system or sanskāras) has been neglected completely, which is essential for the sustenance and survival of man, society, and nature. Until the time, artha (materialism) is governed by dharma (value system or sanskāras), we shall not be able to create a harmonious and peaceful world free from crisis. Dharma, in fact, is a knowledge and comprehension of those eternal principles which govern both nature and humanity, those immutable laws which in one sphere are called 'science' in another 'true philosophy'. It concerns itself not with things true under certain conditions or at certain times: its precepts are ever true, true in the past, true in present, true in future. Thus, truth is the basis for both dharma and science. In Vedic times, science and dharma went hand in hand. However, today dharma is replaced by religion and it has become a settled law that religion and science cannot go hand in hand. The fact is that science without dharma is blind and dharma without science is lame. That is the reason why the modern era facing crisis, troubles and tribulations. The need is to revive the lost Vedic dharma (value system) which is the only solution to the present crisis, moral, cultural, political and environmental as well. The present book discusses in detail the world moral crisis from the Vedic perspective. It is a collection of scholarly articles published in various issues of Vedic Science journal from time to time addressing the key issues haunting the modern society in the light of the Vedic value system.

Dr. Ravi Prakash Arya

Significance of Values in Life

In the name of individual freedom and progressivism though we have been making substantial strides in taking humankind to new heights, but in that blind race, we have become automatons without being concerned for others. We have enthused selfishness in the new generation and call it the only path for individual development i.e. success. In the name of religion and politics, we start wars and do irreparable damage to humankind.

The whole world seems to be in turmoil. The whole fabric of social life seems to have broken. Families are falling apart. There is no respect among various components of human groups, making survival difficult. Nations continuously engage themselves in a war against each other and within nations, one ethnic group tries to weigh down others to maintain its superiority. In families, generations fight in the name of the generation gap, individuals try usurping what may be termed as others' rights. These problems could be solved only by inculcating human values in the present as well as in the coming generations. Only the right values can assure the survival of humanity.

Human values differentiate human beings from animals. According to Vedic tradition **human-being minus human value = Animal**. The word value has been represented in the Vedas and ancient Sanskrit literature by *Dharma*. That is why it was a common paradigm in ancient Indian culture:

dharmeṇa vihinaḥ paśu.

That is, a human being devoid of *Dharma* is no better than an animal.

Just as material things are evaluated in terms of money, human beings are evaluated in terms of moral and spiritual values. Unfortunately, in the modern commercial scientific age, the life of human beings is also valued in terms of money. If somebody dies in an accident or becomes prey to a natural disaster or some catastrophe, his death is compensated with money. That is only a remedy available in the modern world to assuage the death of human beings. Nevertheless, human life is priceless and no money can compensate it. In the Vedic system, the value of life was attached to moral traits often defined as *Dharma*. *Dharma*, according to Manu, the first lawgiver of mankind, is constituted of ten prominent values. They are, *Dhṛti* (patience), *kṣmā* (forgiveness), *dama* (control of mind), *asteyam* (non-stealing), *śauca* (cleanliness), *indriyanigraha* (control of sense organs), *dhi* (intellect), *vidyā* (education), *satyam* (truthfulness), and *akrodha* (non-anger). These values are necessary for human beings. More values, the more refined human-being, fewer values, less refined is the human being. The real personality is defined in light of the above values. In modern times, the concept of personality is based upon persona meaning mask. Accordingly, personality is what appears to be and not what really is. On the other hand, as per Vedic concept, personality is what really is and not what appears to be. The other way round, in Vedic terms, the character makes a man perfect, however, in modern terms, a tailor makes a man perfect.

The Vedas have always played a role of staunch advocate for *Dharma* (set of moral, ethical, cultural, educational and human values) for the Individual and society. The establishment of real *dharma* is possible with the value-based system, instead of value-free system. Today *dharma* is defined as a religion. But *dharma* cannot be religion. Religion is different and *Dharma* is different. Religion is more or less a set of rituals and dogmas, but *dharma* is a set of values. So, both concepts stand poles apart. Swami Dayananda Sarasvati, founder of Arya Samaj movement in India and an embodiment of Vedic life and thought, says while expounding one of the ten principles of Arya Samaj, "Everybody should act according to *dharma*." He defines *dharma* as truth, and truth is the basis of science. As such, *dharma* is the basis of science, whereas religion is anti-science. That is why the people are forced to observe that religion and science cannot go together.

The role of *dharma* (values) in life is quite positive, but the role of religion is quite negative and destructive. Dharma is a uniting force, but religion has become a cause of separation and hatred. Today it has become the root cause of all sorts of conflicts in the world. It is the main cause of terrorism, bloodshed and anarchy. *Dharma* is necessary for global peace, friendship and fraternity.

Vedas are great sourcebooks that advocate values for the smooth, peaceful and trouble-free individual, family, social, economic and political life on this planet. These values are to be inculcated not by way of education and Sanskāras. Vedic value-based society defines leaders not from a political or social point of view but from the point of taking a lead role for the cause of establishment of values in the society and state. A leader is a leader by nature. He cannot become so by education, training or title.

Some of the values advocated in Vedas are as follows: cleanliness, order, discipline, decorum and decency, patience, humility, integrity, honesty, truthfulness, right attitude towards women, leadership, social justice, co-operation, sympathy, love, self realization, right attitude towards other countries and communities, right attitude towards one's own country and its inhabitants, charity, forgiving, propakāra and non-violence.

The Vedas (*Taittirīya Upaniṣad),* emphasize the regular study of Śāstras and Vedas - *svādhyāyo'dhyetavya,* i.e. one must not leave the study of Vedas and allied texts. The influence of reading books on the personality, particularly on growing minds has also been well recorded by modern thinkers like Jean Jacques Rousseau, Amos Bronson Alcott and other scholars. Under the circumstances, the Vedas are a book that fills up the gap. It is the duty of parents, teachers, human institutions, and our policymakers to put their concerted efforts for the betterment of the new generation by inculcating values, otherwise, we are doomed to create a society looking human but deprived of humanity and human beings.

Redefine the Role of Science

To achieve the above-cited objective, it is also essential to redefine the role of science, as the modern age is the age of Science. Science has played a pivotal role in the making of modern society by way of developing the technological know-how. In other words, the main thrust of modern science has been the *sanskāra* of material things. The modern technique of refinement, modification, purification and processing the material things is known in Vedic science as *saṁskāra.* So, we can say that modern science has given stress upon the *sanskāra* of material things and developed a technology to promote the convenience and comfort of human beings. Here there is a basic difference in the concept of Vedic Science and modern science. Vedic science includes the *sanskāra* of human beings primarily while going to the sanskāra of material things. According to Vedic science, a human being who has not gone through the certain process of *sanskāras* remains in his crude form and is recognized as no better than an animal. As such, a human being is not considered to be the actual social being. Just as the material things cannot be used efficiently so long as they are in their crude form, similarly a human being without undergoing the process of Sanskāras, cannot become a social, cultural and civilised being. For their practical application, the material things are subjected to a particular process of refinement or *sanskāra.* For instance, an oil in its crude form cannot be used, but after undergoing the process of refinement it becomes usable. Thus, the conversion of oil from its crude form to the refined form is known as Science. Similarly, the processing of other material things for the use of human-beings is also known as Science. In the race for developing technology, modern Science has totally ignored the need for *saṁskāra* of humans. That is why, today in the age of machinery, human beings are also considered as good as machines. They are equated with life less things and so there is always a talk of human resource development and never as human development. The concept of human resource development is embedded in the very philosophy that gives human beings no better value than other natural resources, which are often exploited for the benefit of an exploiter and so are human beings. However, there is a basic difference between the exploitation of natural sources and the exploitation of human resources. The exploitation of natural resources takes place uniformly for benefit of humanity at large. But so far as human beings are concerned, the poor and weak are exploited by the powerful and rich.

So, Vedas are more concerned about the *saṁskāra* of human beings as compared to the *sanskāra* of material things. Vedic seers never considered human beings as the resource or means, but ends. Everything is directed towards the development and elevation of human beings.

Moreover, Vedic seers have a humanitarian and ethical approach to everything. Their main aim was to relieve human beings permanently of the suffering, social injustice, deprivation and all such problems as were haunting them.

Modern Science has though developed so many aids for the comfort of human beings, yet it has a limited approach. Its approach is not Universal. Modern science has no moral, ethical or humanitarian foundation. It is founded on the laws of survival of fittest in the struggle that ensues among human beings on the globe. Modern science wants to define and describe everything in the light of struggle. It has no remedy to put an end to this struggle. Contrary to this, the main aim of Vedic science is to put an end to this struggle and prepare a stage for peace, friendship, fraternity and co-existence of each and every being on the Earth. It clears a stage for the co-existence of each and every human being by giving a call for accepting the principles of mutual understanding and co-operation among human beings.

saha nāvavatu nau bhunaktu saha vīryaṁ karvāvahai
tejasvināvadhitamastu, mā vidviṣāvahai.

"Let there be co-operation in protection, eating and

gaining power. Let each one of us become illumined with knowledge. let us not envy or struggle with each other."

Since modern science has its foundation laid out on the laws of struggle its talk about the exploitation of natural as well as human resources aims at the comfort of those who are able to survive the struggle on the globe. We can see that in spite of high advancement in the area of technology and production of each and everything, the benefits are not reaching to each and every human being on the globe due solely to the absence of moral and humanitarian values. We have more than a sufficient amount of food grains piled up in our stocks, still, there is poverty and hunger on the globe. At one hand, the excess food grains are being disposed off in the sea, on the other hand, human-beings and other animate beings are dying of hunger. Science has though blessed modern humanity with great prosperity, still, more than 50% of human beings on the globe are below the poverty line and suffering from hunger, thrust, malnutrition, the phenomenon of coldness and hotness, and a dearth of essential things for their survival. One can say unhesitatingly that modern science has failed in performing the *sanskāra* of human beings. It could develop and devise machines but not real human beings.

Today, everything is commercialized. In the blind race of commercialization, moral values have left far behind. Money makes the mare of material advancement go at the cost of moral, ethical, cultural and human values which are, perhaps, the real basis of the advancement of humanity on the globe. These moral values are called by *Vedic* seers as *Dharma.* Since these values are sustaining human life on the globe, so a Vedic seer repeatedly proclaims: *Dhāraṇāt Dharma prāhuḥ.* Dharma is so-called because it sustains humanity and the universe.

There is clear cut observation in the Vedic philosophy that every human being is born as *śudra* (without values) from the womb of his / her mother. After undergoing the process of *saṁśkāra* (values), he becomes *dvija* (twice-born).

janmamā jāyate śudraḥ

saṁśkāraiḥ dvija juccyate.

That is a human-being born physically is not better than an animal. It is the *saṁśkāra* (inculcation of moral values and education) that makes him a real being.

For being the actual human being, one has to take second birth, in addition to his physical birth from the mother's womb, from his *Ācārya's* (Guru's) womb. *Ācārya* (Guru) is a person who educates him and helps him inculcation of moral, cultural and humanitarian values. It is said:

Acārya kasmāt ācinoti arthān ācāram grāhayatīti sataḥ.

Achārya is he who inculcates in his disciple sanskāra of knowledge, good manners, ethical, moral and cultural values.

Just like a child stay for nine months in his / her mother's womb, similarly, he has to stay with *ācārya* in *Gurukula* for years to be born again as a perfect, knowledgeable social human-being. The stay of a child with *ācārya* is called as *antaḥvāsa* and the child observing *antaḥvāsa* (staying in the womb of *ācārya*) is known as *antaḥvāsī.* Just as in developing a certain instrument or machine, several types of processing is required, similarly, in developing a perfect human being, the Vedic sages stressed the need for sixteen *saṁśkāras* right from the birth till death of an individual. The advancement of modern science is lop-sided. It has developed a perfect machinery, but failed to develop a perfect human being.

So far, we have confined ourselves to the physical and mental *saṁśkāra* of the human beings and so for maintaining the physical health, researches are going on, but for the upkeep and maintenance of moral health or character-building, no research or effort has been put in. Whereas Vedic scientist was equally concerned about the moral health (education and character building) as was about the physical and mental health.

Vedic ideas are still very much relevant for the upkeep and advancement of modern society. In times of need, even today, is also the moral and spiritual education, inculcation of ethical, moral and humanitarian values and spiritual advancement, so that the modern society may rid of vices of struggle, exploitation, commercialisation of each and every thing and may be endowed with moral / humanitarian and spiritual values, so that all human beings may become perfect human beings (*Āryas)* and remove hunger, poverty, deprivation from the globe through their mutual co-operation, instead of being compartmentalized and divided along the lines of caste, race, creed, region and religion. Let the whole world sing the Vedic song.

Bhumi mātā putro'ahaṁ pṛthivyāḥ

"Earth is my mother and I am the child of mother earth."

World Moral Crisis
(A Vedic Perspective)

A powerful nation as well as a fanatic group can wage a war, not only with impunity but with moral certitude! Multinationals exploit lesser developed nations for 'profit' and spread ill health's well! The whole of nature is being exploited, as though, under attack from a sworn enemy, and endangers the entire environment! The world is undergoing a moral crisis, only a few (wise) feel so!

The subject of ethics has been complex and confusing no doubt, but now it is confounded. There are conflicts between man and nature, man and man, man and woman, man and child, even between husband and wife, between parents and children! Society has been disintegrated, now the power-hungry and greedy are calling the shots. Thinking is 'not allowed'. Media keeps people entangled in baser emotions and trivia of models, actors and players. Man is being converted into a consuming machine, a zombie. Even house-wives and college girls are into flash trade. Politicians also do not encourage thinking; and manage votes by roadshows or threats. Are these the signs of a society happily submerged in the bottomless ocean of consumerism, or can we take these as warning signals of a society getting into a quagmire? Should it not make some of us ponder over the painfully pathetic primitive passions that we are a prisoner of? Are we living in a world of moral poverty amidst plenty of pleasures?

What are we being driven by in our lives, by instincts that are common with beasts or by ideals that are divine? Humans are capable of becoming a demon or divine. Chasing to satisfy the base passions we dehumanize ourselves, and by making the world a happy place we fulfill the divine in ourselves.

Do we want to make this world a happy place by fulfilling the needs of all and discovering the font of happiness within? But why should we make this world a happy place, and not just enjoy ourselves? After all, everyone is responsible for himself? This is the most fundamental question which metaethics attempts to answer.

Religions were the first to attempt to answer this question. Semitic religions claim that their prophets have had revelations in their mystic visions, which are given as commandments. Whosoever follows these, such as, love they neighbour, do not kill, be not be greedy etc, would please the God and ascend to heaven on the Day of judgment. The commandments ordain values to control the animal in the men and encourage the noble in him. But apart from blind faith, why should anybody obey these religious commandments! After all, the fight within for self-interest against altruism goes on, in which generally self-interest wins. Even morals such as 'love thy neighbour' are justified on the basis that you would be loved by your neighbour then. Thus this noble principle is also justified by self-interest, a utilitarian concept[1], which has its own shortcomings. These days science and technology have loosened the hold of faith, and more so blind faith, significantly in western countries; and have failed to provide convincing humane ethics. This is one of the causes of the present miserable condition of the world today.

Western philosophers have also attempted to develop ethics. They can be divided into two major groups. One group recommends objective values also known as 'otherworldly' values. Plato was the first one to define them as eternal, absolute and universal. They are not man-made, for they reside in the 'spirit – realm.' It may be noted that these values are non- subjective and not objective in the scientific sense. Here again morals, for acceptance, need **faith** in the wisdom of the philosopher-king.

The other group was led by 'skeptics', who believed that

---

[1] Arthur Schopenhauer

values are subjective and not objective. Their school of thought is also known as 'this-worldly' school. Their system of ethics is 'culture -- relative', and thus may be individual and/or society -- relative. Culture -- relative ethics was propounded by the Greek philosopher Sextus Empiricus, and later on developed by Hume, Immanuel Kant, Michelle Montaigne, William Graham Sumner etc. This is further divided into two groups. Hume propounded anti-rational or emotion-based ethics; and Kant the rational -- ethics. Hume believed that values cannot be based on logic, they are accepted or rejected by heart. Rationalist Kant proposed that values have to be decided logically, as those based on the heart's acceptance may not be consistent and universal. Values have to be decided 'a priori', i.e. developed logically based on a set of axioms. He proposed the concept of 'categorical imperative', i.e. absolute commandment, viz. 'men must be treated as an end, and not as an instrument. Man's real value is intrinsic and not instrumental. This certainly is a golden rule, but if somebody denies it, then no logic can be given to convince him otherwise, except faith in the axiom.

Western psychologists of the 'egoist' school have stated that basically a man is motivated by self-interests viz. preservation, propagation and pleasure. Hedonists among these state that fulfilment of one's desires, especially those for pleasures are the basic drives of a man. It is obvious that if everybody is motivated by such desires, then there would be clashes. The only answer that hedonists have is to limit the circle of one's desires so that they do not clash with others, or the one who succeeds in the competition would fulfil his desires at the cost of others. Thus, it can be seen that this set of values would lead to clashes and miseries. The more powerful would dominate, and exploit the weaker.

Bantham and Mills proposed 'Utilitarianism' as the basis of ethics. This also has many difficulties, the worst being the definition of 'utility' itself. Even an innocent definition like 'well being of many' can be used to justify slavery.

Briefly speaking, all the western systems of ethics ultimately depend upon an axiom or a divine commandment, and thus on belief or faith. Today, in this age of science and technology, belief or faith is losing its hold in the western world. With the loss in faith or belief, Western religions do not have any credible mechanism for the control of consumerism, except asceticism. The only argument in favour of asceticism is that their religious book ordains that an ascetic would reach heaven on the Day of Judgment, which again is a matter of pure faith.

Basis of the Vedic Ethical System: Vedic ethics is not only a symbiosis of all the systems of western ethics, but transcends them all. Vedas state that ethics is absolute, eternal and universal, and yet is verifiable. Any person can verify this, provided he follows certain procedure called 'Sādhanā', and is thus not restricted to a rare prophet. The 'Sādhanā' takes its practitioner to the fourth state of consciousness, called '*turīya*' or transcendental state, beyond waking, dreaming and deep sleep. In such a state, one is aware of 'existence' of '*Ānanda*' (bliss), and nothing else. He also realizes who he really is, i.e. he is that 'consciousness' which in Sanskrit is known as '*Sachchidānanda*', and also as '*Brahman*', the ultimate Reality. He realizes that this cosmos is his-Self, there is nothing else but that Consciousness. This is also termed as 'Brahman' or the Supreme Being, which is both transcendental and immanent. This experience is not a revelation, but a realization. A realized person loves others as his-Self, he does not hate anybody because there is no other. It is difficult, if not impossible, to describe that transcendental experience. If a person owns, say, ten cars, he would like all of them, though he may have preferences depending upon their utility for different purposes. Similar is the case with a realized person. This experience of spiritual, mental and physical non-duality is the basis or metaethics of Vedic ethics. Anyone can experience it. Ramakrishna, Vivekanand, Maharshi Raman, Swami Dayanand Saraswati, Aurobindo, etc. are modern examples of such realized persons.

What is an axiom to Kant, the categorical imperative, or what exists in the 'spirit realm' for Plato is an experiential realization to a seeker. Vedic ethics thus is both 'otherworldly' and 'this-worldly', is both rationalistic and anti-rationalistic, and even more. Two main principles flow from such a realization. First is the absolute unity in the cosmos, the existence of nothing but Brahman. Therefore 'love all' is the first principle. The second principle states that the purpose of all humans is to realize this bliss, the ultimate source of happiness because in any case, all are striving for happiness. A realized person is an intrinsically happy person and therefore does not crave for physical and mental pleasures. Consumerism is not the goal of his life. It becomes his nature to help seekers towards realization. It does not mean that a realized person renounces this world. As described in Upanishads, e.g, in the eleventh mantra of *Īśāvāśya Upaniṣad*, 'a person is very much required to live in it and look after the worldly needs as well'. One of the main causes of misery, cruelty, etc. is the consuming and destructive competition between individuals, between groups, religions, nations, etc. Vedic ethics, by removing such differences, cuts at the root of the problem.

It is often said that both God and ethics are man-made, they are inventions of humankind. Vedic transcendental experience removes the very basis of such a concept.

The principles of Vedic ethics are equally applicable to all, irrespective of their colour, creed, caste or gender, etc. The principles are humanitarian, as love, truth, non-violence, etc are fundamental values to be human. Not only does a Vedic seeker sees unity everywhere, but he also sees that different persons may see the same truth differently - "*ekam sad viprāḥ bahudhā vadanti*" ! And it also advises that all statements of no single authority need to be authentic. Vedic thought declares that other persons can have their truth. Everyone has a right to his truth. Thus Vedic ethics is not exclusivists and not deontological. Cultural-relativism is in-built in Vedic ethics but at the same time, it maintains that 'Reality' is universal, absolute and eternal. Principles of Vedic ethics are useful without being 'utilitarian'. From consciousness, bliss and existence logically and existentially flow other values like love, truth, non-violence, service, wisdom, fortitude, forgiveness, control of mind and sensual apparatus, non-theft, non-greed, non-anger, knowledge, etc. etc.

Consumerism, the mother of most of the miseries, loses its raison d'etre because one realizes that one's body is his vehicle for the journey of life, and therefore needs to be looked after, but only as an instrument needs to be looked after. The first mantra of *Īśāvāsya* is relevant which logically commends to enjoy with full detachment, '*tena tyaktena bhuñjithāḥ*'. Further, there are four major steps (*puruṣārtha*) of action in the journey of life - viz. *dharma* (values and guiding principles of life), *artha* (resources), *kāma* (desires) and *mokṣa* (liberation). Resources or wealth is to be earned ethically and only for the purpose of fulfilling desires approved by the ethics, at the same time aiming for *mokṣa*, i.e. liberation from miseries. Such principles, being based on oneness and love, would encourage co-operation as against competition, need-based consumption as against unlimited consumption. This leads to the principle of behaviour - 'do unto others as you want them to do unto you.'

Most of the ethical principles of any school are considered noble by most of us for most of the time. But then why do we fail to apply them in our life? There are many reasons, but probably the most important is a lack of full conviction in their authenticity, if they depend upon faith or belief. Lack of faith or belief in ethical values supports consumerism and hunger for power, which in turn supports the lack of faith or belief! Thus a vicious circle has formed and terrorism, consumption, destructive competition and clashes, etc. are increasing misery despite the increase in unprecedented benefits of science and technology. Vedic ethics, for a seeker, begins with one hundred percent conviction. Those who have no time for realization, have to have faith. The fact that the fundamental principles of Vedic ethics can be verified is in itself a reassuring factor. This happens all the time in science. Most of us have not seen electrons or protons, but we believe in their existence because their existence has been verified by scientists, and is open to verification by anybody.

The process of reform should begin with the mind. The preamble of UNESCO declares that wars begin in the minds of people, therefore we should purify the mind first. Vedic ethics also begins with the mind. That is why for the western way of living 'global village' is a market phenomenon, but in Vedic ethics, it is '*vasudhaiva kuṭumbakam*' a family phenomenon.

Tackling of terrorism, as per Vedic ethics, would demand the spread of message of love, truth and unity, as Gandhi had done. As a last resort use of force or was is not ruled out, as was recommended by Krishna in Gītā.

The perennial problem of poverty needs to be handled not only on the economic front but also ethically. It is very important that poverty and any weakness is not to be exploited, which needs deep empathy, and the same is in-built in Vedic ethics. Reduction in consumption would save the earth, save the future and also the poor. Thus conservation of mother nature is also in-built in Vedic ethics. Plants, trees, forest, insects, fishes, mammals, etc. are all part of the same one family because we are all intrinsically the same. Vedic ethics has been practiced more or less in India for a long time, although many instances can be quoted when Indians have not exercised gender, religious, and caste equality. Given the human nature, that should not be surprising. What is pleasantly surprising is that many more instances can also be quoted when Hindus have exercised the principle of equality. Gārgī debated with the great sage Yājñalkya in the court of King Janaka; Kaikeyī used to accompany Daśaratha to battlefields; Sītā went to the forest with Rāma despite opposition from all concerned; tribal leader Niṣāda, Vānara (Mongoloid) leaders Sugrīva and Hanumāna, etc. were treated by Rāma with equal love and dignity. India has produced women queens, saints, poetesses, etc. during the middle ages. Jews have publicly declared that it is only in India that they have never been persecuted. Parsees (Persian refugees) have lived amicably for more than a thousand years in India as Indians. Muslims are not known for their tolerance, but for a long time, Hindus have lived with them in a friendly manner.

One more important crisis in the world must be considered, and that is the lack of scientific temper amongst the people of the world, including Europe and the USA. The unscientific attitude of Christians is well known from the burning at the stake of Bruno, banishment of Tyco Brahe, house arrest of Galileo, verbal attack on Darwin, etc. As a consequence the concept of secularism was created in the West. Even today in the USA, Darwin's theory cannot be taught in many schools unless creation theory as in the Bible is also taught. Today, about 50% of persons in the USA believe in ghosts, communication with dead persons, etc. Vedic ethics, as has been shown, is scientific in a broader sense and encourages free and rational thinking, though giving due importance to intuition at the same time, through tolerance and questioning any authority. Vedic system of thought convinces that both scientific progress and spiritual progress are essential in this world for a happy life.

We see that the philosophy in the Vedic thoughts is firstly humanistic and worldly. It convinces, through realization, that love, truth, non-violence, equality, and justice, etc. are essential for happiness. Consumerism is destructive and causes misery in the world. Tolerance and open-minded approach are necessary for a peaceful life. Realization of *Sat-Cit-Ānanda* (Existence - Consciousness - Bliss) should be the primary goal of life, which then automatically leads to a happy life for all. It prays for happiness of all, not of one sect or nation, as can be seen in one of its prayers - 'may all be happy; may all be healthy; may all experience nobility; may nobody suffer unhappiness. *Lokāḥ samastaḥ sukhino bhavantu.*

Values! Where to find them?

Etymologically, the word 'value' is derived from the French word 'valoir' meaning ' be worth' (The New Shorter Oxford Dictionary, 1993). This meaning has an economical tinge. The same implication is found in the definition given by James Drever (Dictionary of Psychology), who defines it as "a quantitative measure of a standard or unit".

Kretch (1962) defines it with human touch as "a belief about what is desirable or good." In the same way, Rokeach (1973) defines it as an "enduring belief that is personally or socially preferable to opposite or converse mode of conduct or a state of existence." W.E.Martin, quoted by Hurlock (1976), defines values as "precipitate of behaviour: they are established predisposition of behaviour"(p.189). They are what is attractive to a person, the essence of what he seeks in an object, a person, or even himself. As such, they operate as criteria for making judgements between alternative courses of action and they directly influence the quality of a person's behaviour and decisions. As a rule, the person adopts those values which help them to achieve the ends he desires and which are at the same time, sanctioned by the group with which he is identified. His values are thus influenced and are a reflection of his personality.

Spranger, quoted by Coleman (1971), describes six types of values: The Theoretical (concerned with the discovery of truth), the Economic (concerned with utility and practical affairs viz. production, marketing, consumption, and material possession of wealth), the Aesthetic (concerned with form and harmony), the social (concerned with affiliation and love), the Political (concerned with power, the focus is on personal relationship in power, influence and active competition to maintain and expand power), and the Religious (concerned with unity, mysticism, and relation with cosmos).

Bayati (1987) gave three kinds of values, naming them as the Instrumental, the Intrinsic and the Aesthetic. The instrumental values are said to be good for something and are subjective and selective to people and situations; the intrinsic values are self-contained and the aesthetic values are subject to intensified appreciation.

Dr. B. Ratnakumari (1991) performed a cluster-analysis of human values and found that except for four value-aspects viz. Faith in Man, Dependability, Sense of Beauty, and Dignity of Labour, other values form two clusters, which may be termed as the value-aspects of the two core values which are:

1. Striving for Excellence, which includes the value aspects of Clear thinking, Courage to face Reality, Personal Conviction, Perseverance, Self-Study, Devotion to Work, Freedom to Act, Sportiveness, Citizenship, Equality, Humility to Accept and Correct Mistakes, Self-Reliance, Adaptability, Appreciating Others, Capabilities, Truthfulness, and Curiosity.

2. Value of Reliability (Concern for Others), which includes the value-aspects of, Courtesy, Sharing, Compassion, Availability, Community-Spirit, Forgiveness, Respect for Others' Rights, Mutual Acceptance, Social Service, National Consciousness, Appreciation for Others, Cultural Values, Co-operation, Readiness to Espouse a Common Cause, and Value for Public Property.

According to Dr. Pandey (1996), the Directorate of Primary and Secondary Education has incorporated the education of 32 life values in its school programme. Even NCERT has drawn a list of 83 values for social, moral, and spiritual development of our future citizens.

The present author's view in this regard is that the basic values are only three: *Satyam, Śivam* and *Sundaram*: truth, goodness and beauty, ultimate elements according to Plato. When they are seen in the context of individual life, family life, community life, national life, human race and the whole cosmos, they intermingle in different ratios and are named differently.

Their absence denotes undesirables.

Truth is the discovery and pursuit of reality in the purest form. Beauty is the realization of the harmony, balance, order and proportion of the structure or configuration, physical, or mental, whatever the case may be. But these absolutes are useless and meaningless if they are pursued for their own sake. Pure truth and beauty may be admired and appreciated as philosophical constructs but they don't affect the quality of human existence. They are there but they do not contribute anything to the welfare and sustenance of human existence. That is why Plato subordinated these under the supreme value of goodness. The goodness or as it is called *Śivam* or *Śreya* in Sanskrit gives the desired congeniality and amiability to the values of truth and beauty in the context of the whole cosmos and particularly in the context of human existence.

When truth is pursued for finding out the essence of existence or reality only, and its sole aim is nothing but finding out the truth only, as a scientific or philosophical principle or law or some mechanism, it leads to Hiroshima and Nagasaki. Similarly, the realization of beauty for beauty's sake only or the quest for absolute beauty may lead one on the path of becoming a Narcissus or an infatuated being lost in the hypothetical constructions and severing its relation with the phenomenal world.

But the subjugation of truth and beauty to goodness make these values humane. This, then, opens the path towards the social structures where human beings work for the attainment of those discoveries that make the life worth living and are related to their welfare and well-being and also work the realization of beauty for giving them a balanced, harmonious, proportionate and ordered model for co-operative living. A human being without goodness will sure become a Nadirshah, a Chengizkhan, or an Adolf Hitler. A Buddha or Gandhi becomes a reality when goodness manifests itself with its force.

According to Sarma (1961), in *Kaṭhopaniṣad*, the distinction between *Śreya* (that which possesses goodness) and *Preya* (having beauty, and lovability or likeability, but not goodness) has been given much thought.

"The good (*Śreya*) is one thing, the pleasant (*Preya*) another. These two, having different purposes, they bind a man. Of these two, it is well for him who takes hold of the good (*Śreya*); he who chooses the pleasant (*Preya*) misses its end".

"The good (*Śreya*) and the pleasant (*Preya*) approach a man, the wise man considers and distinguishes between the two. Wisely does he prefer the good (*Śreya*) to the pleasant (*Preya*), but a fool chooses the pleasant (*Preya*) for its worldly good."

The goodness or *Śreya* is the ultimate value for the individual as well as for the society at large. Without this value other values become evils. To illustrate my point, I may say that I will not return the sword that I borrowed from someone, who has presently gone mad; lest it may harm someone. Although it is the right thing that whatever has been borrowed from one must be returned to him. Dishonesty, exploitation, animosity, unhealthy competition, corruption, etc. are indicative of the lack of goodness and beauty in personal and social relationships. Going to the other side, we find that respect for others, beliefs, good manners, discipline, honesty, compassion, kindness, etc. are the virtues having goodness and beauty in them. That is the reason why competitiveness, success, and riches become evils when these are devoid of goodness value in them.

Human life develops from a cell. We do not know the effects of the mother's values on the ovum, embryo, and foetus yet. Anyway the newborn child is certainly under the influence of its mother. Those who surround it, have active interaction with it and stimulate and guide it in its behaviour. The child, at first, culls the information, which it receives through its sense organs, on the basis of the impact it provides, be it pleasant or unpleasant, and reacts to it in the form of a limited number of behaviour patterns available to it. Slowly, it begins to imitate the language, gestures, and attitudes towards things and persons also.

Through the same process, the growing child imbibes the values inherent in its environment. And we must remind ourselves that nowadays our environment does not consist of few simple things and uncomplicated relationships among parents, peers, and some other persons only, as it was the case in not so far past, but also of Shaktimans, Tendulkars, Jadejas, Kroor Singhs, Osama bin Ladens, Kajols, Amir Khans, Martandokars, Bendres, Bipasha Basus, etc. When it is a little more grown-up, it begins to imitate the language styles, dress, vocabulary, hairstyle of those, who influence him most. You may agree with me or not, but I am of the view that such actions play havoc with the inculcation of really desirable values in him/her. Even the mother, who shows the preference for a particular child for wrong reasons, a father, who asks the child to lie, or a teacher, who awards a child spurious grades, puts the child on the path of undesirable values, which affects its own life as well as the society at large for the years to come.

The only hope lies if the parents, teachers, human institutions, and our policymakers combine their efforts - and work for the betterment of the new generation, otherwise we are doomed to create a society looking human but deprived of human values. I think the good literature can play a part in the process because literature is the mirror of society. A mirror shows distorted images if it is dusty, or curved, or scratches over it. The object itself, if it is not clean or pure, may create an image unworthy of being emulated. The condition is that we must put before the child, who is a part of a growing generation, a picture or image that is capable of inspiring him. In the name of realism, we have put examples before the new generation that creates pessimism in it about the human existence. Sure, we can make a demon image out of clay, yet a good artist can always make figures worthy of attention and appreciation. I don't think that as human beings we should escape from realities but this is also of utmost importance that we should put before the growing minds good images of human conduct and not prematurely, stuff their minds with the obnoxious and gory images found in society. Coleridge, the poet, said, "There is too much beauty on this earth for a lonely man to bear." Yet, we see only ugly and distorted scenes and miss the sunrise for mud. As mature persons we can afford that, but if young minds see only ugly things and experience undesirable behaviour they are sure to loose sight of all that is beautiful in the surroundings.

The books also play a vital role in shaping our personalities.

"Plutarch presently became my greatest favourite. The satisfaction I derived from repeated readings I gave this author, extinguished my passion for romances, and I shortly preferred Agesilaus, Brutus, and Aristides, to Orondates, Artemenes, and Juba. These interesting studies seconded by the conversations they frequently occasioned with my father, produced that republican spirit and love of liberty, that haughty and invincible turn of mind, which rendered me impatient of restraint or servitude, and became the torment of my life, as I continually found myself in situations incompatible with these sentiments. Incessantly occupied with Rome or Athens, conversing, if I may so express myself with their illustrious heroes; born as the citizen of a republic, of a father whose ruling passion was a love for his country, I was fired with these examples; could fancy myself a Greek or Roman, and readily give into the character of the personage whose life I read; transported by the recital of any extraordinary instance of fortitude or intrepidity, animation flashed from my eyes, and gave my voice additional strength and energy. One day, at table, while relating fortitude of Scoevola, they were terrified at seeing me start from my seat and hold my hand over a hot chafing-dish, to represent more forcibly the action of that determined Roman."

"That is a good book," wrote Amos Bronson Alcott, "which is opened with expectation, and closed with delight and profit." According to Ernest Heming way, "All good books are alike in that they are truer than if they had really happened and after you are finished reading one you will feel that all that happened to you and afterwards it all belongs to you; the good and the bad, the ecstasy, the remorse and sorrow, the people and the places and how the weather was."

My point is that by reading good books we can transform our nature and that is a process, which must be used for the inculcation of good values in our children. No doubt, time tested books must be used for this purpose, and that too, with much caution.

The influence of bad books and undesirable information on the young mind is often responsible for crimes. When a boy, with the help of his friends, murders his mother, as happened in New Delhi, for the money he needs to satisfy his not-so-normal desires, or when a father rapes his own daughters, we can not dismiss the cases as exceptions. The malady lies deep in the form of wrong and undesirable wants, created by bad examples and bad readings.

In India, our two great historical epics, *Vālmīki Rāmāyaṇa* and *Mahābhārata* have been used for making people understand the complexities of different minds and the solution to various problems that come with them. In the history of *Mahābhārata*, we find two groups of people, of the same clan, fighting a cold war that results in a great war destroying everything. It happened because one group wished to take away the just rights of the other group, and seniors felt helpless because of their affection towards the first group. Only the *dharma* was the guiding spirit for people of the other group and in the last, they won. This historical epic is for mature minds, who are not lured away with the fallacious arguments of the unjust group. The characters mainly belong to royal families, and the common people, if they are there, who are for the menial tasks.

In contrast, the *Vālmīki Rāmāyaṇā*, through the History of Rama, the heir apparent of Ayodhya's throne, have plenty of common people, who take part in the discussions, exploits, and policy-making, and sometimes seem to be at par with the hero. Even Rama, for fourteen long years of his exile, is not treated or depicted as a mighty king but like a hermit, who mingles with the individuals and groups of sub-human races at equal footing. Tulsidas, the author of *Rāmcaritamānas*, noted down this quality of Rama in the following couplet:

prabhu tarutar kapi dar par, so kiye āpu samānā.
Tulsi katahun na rāma so, sahab, sīla nidhānā.

"Rama is sitting under the tree, and monkeys are there up in the branches, yet Rama treats them as his equals. Tulsidas says that there is none like Rama, as a master full of virtuous character."

Jawaharlal Nehru in his *Discovery of India*, wrote about the two epics as follows:

"I do not know any book anywhere which has exercised such a continuous and pervasive influence on the mass-minds as these two. Dating back to a remote antiquity, they are still a living force in the life of Indian people." (Quoted by N. Chandrasekhara Aiyar in Indian Inheritance (vol.1, p. 27).

Now I shall discuss the values of discipline and sense of beauty as dealt with in the ancient texts of India.

Discipline

According to the meanings of the word 'discipline' provided by NSOD, most of the meanings seem to have a negative undertone. For example, it is chastisement or correction undergone as a penance or self-mortification; it is moral progression brought about by adversity; it is training in military exercises; it is controlled and orderly behaviour resulting from training; it is the system of order and strict obedience to rules enforced among pupils, soldiers, or others under authority. Indians believed in self-discipline. Repression was permitted in extreme cases. *Cāṇakya-nīti* permitted the chastisement of children only between the ages of five and sixteen, before five and after sixteen years it was not permitted. Bible says, 'Discipline your children while they are young enough to learn. If you don't, you are helping to destroy themselves'. (Proverbs, 19.18)

According to Coleman (1971), '...lack of discipline tends to produce a spoiled, inconsiderate, anti-social and aggressive child. On the other hand, harsh or overly severe discipline may have a variety of effects, including fear and hatred of the punishing person, little initiative or spontaneity, and a lack of friendly feelings towards others.' (p.120)

But Indians believed that discipline was necessary for self-realisation. The Sanskrit word for discipline is *anuśāsana*. The whole of *Yoga*-philosophy is based on disciplining the body and mind. It is said in a revered treatise '*atha yogānuśāsnam'*. (*Pātañjala-yoga-pradipa*, *Samādhipāda*, 1), meaning thereby that we now begin to explain the procedure or method of disciplining the body and mind, which is called *yoga*. It comprises of eight steps viz. *yama*, *niyama*, *āsana*, *prāṇāyāma*, *pratyāhāra*, *dhāraṇā*, *dhyāna*, and *samādhi*. According to Agrawal (1965 : p. 90), *yama* means restraint, *niyama* is discipline or to live according to prescribed rules, of course in a restricted sense, *āsana* is posture, *prāṇāyāma* is control of breathing mechanism, *pratyāhāra* is withdrawal or returning back, *dhāraṇā* is fixed attention, *dhyāna* is contemplation, and *samādhi* is upright meditation. In a mild sense, discipline is to follow one's instruction or live a thoroughly regulated life.

In *VR*. we find most of the characters quite disciplined. There are moments when Lakṣmaṇa, the younger brother of Rāma expresses his opinion that seems unrestrained and yet under the influence of the advice and suggestion of Rāma he does what may be called as most disciplined acts. It makes the depiction of human.

There are many instances of disciplinary conduct throughout *VR*.. yet the most poignant one is related with Rāma's acceptance of the two conditions prescribed by Kaikeyī, his stepmother, Bharata's mother.

It is quite difficult for anyone, who was to accept the reigns of a kingdom, to be told that he is now to go to exile for fourteen years as a hermit, but Rāma is made of altogether a different material and behaves like not an ordinary son or mortal.

Rāma has entered the chamber of his stepmother where Daśaratha, his father, is lying in a confused state of mind, dejected and miserable state. Rāma asks Kaikeyī the reason for this. Kaikeyī tells Rāma :

eṣaḥ mahyaṁ varaṁ datvā purā māmabhipūjya ca
sa paścāt tapyate rājā yathānyaḥ prakṛtastathā.
(Ayodhyākāṇḍa,18.22)

Having granted me a boon in the past and (thereby) honoured me, this illustrious monarch now repents in the same way as any other common man. (22)

atisṛjya dadāniti varaṁ mām viśāmpatiḥ
sa nirarthaṁ gatjale setum banditumicchati. (Ayo.18.23)

Having given a pledge to me in the words 'I grant you a boon' the celebrated monarch seeks in vain to construct a dam across a stream whose water has already flown. (23)

yadi tvabhihitaṁ rājan tvayi tanna vipatśyate
tato ahamabhidhāsyāmi na hyeṣa tvayi vakṣyati.
(Ayo.18.26)

In case that has been uttered by the king does not fall flat on you, then alone I shall give it out to you. In no case is he is going to open his lips before you. (26)

etat tu vacanam śrutvā Kaikeyyā samudāhṛtam
uvāca vyathito Ramastaṁ deviṁ nṛpa-sannidhau
(Ayo.18.27)

aho dhiṅg nārhase devi vaktuṁ māmidṛśam vacaḥ
ahaṁ hi vacanād rajñaḥ pateyamapi pāvake
(Ayo.18.28.)

bhakṣyeyam viṣam tikṣṇam pateyamapi caraṇau
niyukto guruna pitrā nṛpen ca hiten ca
(Ayo.*18.29)*

tad brūhi vacanaṁ devi rajñoḥ ya5d abhikāṅkṣitam
kariṣye pratijāne ca Ramodvirnabhibhāṣate (Ayo.*18.30)*

Distressed to hear the aforementioned words uttered by Kaikeyī, Sri Rāma for his part spoke (as follows) to the said queen in the presence of the emperor (27).

Oh how shameful (it is for me to hear such words expressing doubt about my devotion to my father)! You ought not to speak such words to me, O glorious lady! At the bidding of my father I am actually prepared to leap into fire.(28)

Commanded by the emperor, who is my teacher, father, and friend, I might as well swallow deadly poison and take a plunge into the ocean. (29)

(Therefore) speak out what you have got to say, O glorious lady! I shall do that which is coveted by the king and give my plighted word (for it), Know that Rāma does not speak twice." (30)

Kaikeyī told Rāma that according to his promise he was to live in the forest for fourteen years and Bharata, her son, was to be consecrated.

tadpṛyamitrājño vacnam marṇopamam
śrutvā na vivyathe Rāmaḥ kaikeyiṁ cedamabravīt

(Ayo.19.1)

evamastu gamiṣyāmi vanam vastumahaṁ tvitaḥ
jataciradhāro rajñaḥ pratijñām anupālyan (Ayo.19.2)

Śrī Rāma, the destroyer of his enemies, did not feel distressed to hear that message, which was (so) unpleasant to hear and was like death (itself), and spoke to Kaikeyī as follows: (1)

A men! Honouring the promise made by the king and wearing matted locks and bark of trees, I will undoubtedly proceed from Ayodhyā to the forest to take up my abode (there). (2)

To his mother Rāma said:

asmākam tu kule pūrvaṁ sāgarasyajñayan pituḥ
khanadbhiḥ-sāgarairbhūmimvasaḥ-umahān-vadhaḥ.

(Ayo.21.32)

A tragic death was met in the past by the sons in the dynasty of Sagara, belonging to our race, while digging the earth under the command of their father. (32)

etair anyaiṣca bahubhir devi devsamaiḥ kṛtam
piturvacanam klibam kariṣyāmi piturhitam (Ayo.21.34)

Their fathers' behest has been unhesitatingly carried out by these as well as by many other godlike men, I (too) shall (therefore) do a good turn to my father. O! godly mother!

Indeed! No such discipline is found, except in the character of Rāma, in any literature, at any time.

There is a psychological principle, often stressed by parenting-experts. It states that if you make a rule for the family members, then it must be strictly observed, and one who disregards it, must be punished or reminded of his mistake.

In *VR.* there are two instances, when Rāma reprimands Lakṣmaṇa, for his disobeying Rāma's order. The first one is just after Sitā's kidnapping by Rāvaṇa. When Rāma went to kill the deer in a golden hue, he tells Lakṣmaṇa :

tvacā pradhāna ya hyeṣa mṛgo adya na bhaviṣ yatiapramatten te bhāvyama āśramasthena sitayā.

(Āraṇya. 43.49)

yāvat pṛṣṭamekena sāyakena nihanmyaham hatvaitatccarma cādaya śighrameṣyāmi Lakṣmaṇa.

(Āranya. *43. 50)*

pradakṣiṇenatibalena pakṣiṇā Jaṭāyuṣā buddhimattā ca Lakṣmaṇā
bhavapramattaḥ pratigṛhya maithiliṁ pratikṣaṇam sarvata eva shaṅkitaḥ.

(Āraṇya. 43. 51)

Indeed this deer will perish today because of its superb skin. You must remain wide awake in the hermitage with Sitā till I punish this spotted deer by killing it with a single arrow and return, O Lakṣmaṇa! (49-50)

Keeping Sītā, a princess of Mithilā, by your side, O Lakṣ maṇa, remain vigilant every moment and full of apprehension from all quarters in the company of the wise Jaṭāyu who used to fly in the sky and is very powerful and possessed of great might. (51)

When Rāma killed Mārīca, the ogre in the disguised form of a golden deer, he screamed calling Lakṣmaṇa, as if Rāma was in danger, Sītā ordered Lakṣmaṇa to go to help him. Because of castigating remarks made by Sītā that he wished to possess her, Lakṣmaṇa very reluctantly left her and went in the direction of the scream. In the meantime, Rāvaṇa carried away Sītā. When Rāma saw Lakṣmaṇa coming, he said:

aho Lakshmana garhyim te kritam yat tvam vihaya tam.
(Araṇya. 57. 17)

Ah Lakṣmaṇa, a reproachful act has been done by you in that you came away here leaving alone Sītā, who deserved protection. (17)

In the same continuation, Rāma uses words like 'you failed in your duty' (58.11) and 'an error which was grievous in every respect has been committed by you, (58.15) and 'An unbecoming act has been committed by you in that you came hither without her' (59.21).

Another such instance is found in *Uttarakāṇḍa.* When Rāma was approached by the Yama, Rāma ordered Lakṣmaṇa to remain at the door, and not permit anyone or himself to enter till the conversation was over. Rāma had said:

sa me vadhyaḥ khalu bhaved vācaṁ dvandva samiratam
ṛṣermam ca saumitre paśyed vā śṛṇuyacca yaḥ.
(Uttar.103.15)

Lakṣmaṇa! Be on guard, for one, who will see me conversing with the sage, or listens to our talk, will be killed by me.

Actually, this was the condition laid by the Yama himself, who had come in the garb of a sage, for talking to Rāma.

In the meantime, Durvāśā, a sage famed for his ire, approached Lakṣmaṇa and wished to meet Rāma, immediately. If delayed, he was to curse the whole kingdom of Ayodhyā, Lakṣmaṇa, Rāma, Bharata, and their progeny. Lakshmana, considering the welfare of others, entered the chamber, and conveyed Durvāsā's message. After seeing off the Yama and placating Durvāsā, Rāma turned towards Lakṣmaṇa, who was ready to face the death sentence and said:

visarjaye tvaṁ Saumitre mā bhūd dharma viparyayaḥ
tyāgo vadho vā vihitaḥ sādhūnām hyabhayam samam.
(Uttar. 106. 13)

I leave you, O son of Sumitrā, in order to save Dharma, desertion, or slaying- both are the same for the pious ones.

This may sound irrational now, but when Rāma ordered the

banishment of Sītā to the forest, no brother objected to it or spoke against it. (*Uttar.* 45). Rāma, himself was convinced of Sītā's chastity, but in order to maintain the ethics in the society and in view of the public allegations, Rāma had to take these hard decisions being the King, as the kings are considered the ideals and trendsetters in the society.

Sense of Beauty

According to John H. Brown in Concise Encyclopaedia of Philosophy (p.79), there are not many points on which the theorists agree, and that too on the rudiments of the term. Realists view is that the judgements of beauty ascribe to their subjects either a non-relational property inherent in things or a capacity of things to affect respondents in a way that preserves objectivity. The adherents of Classical Platonism hold that beauty exists as an ideal super-sensible form. Eighteenth-century theorists view it as a quasi-sensory property. According to Kant's transcendental philosophy, the experience of beauty depends upon the requirements of cognition, having subjective universality and necessity. The reality is that western philosophical tradition has never developed any theory of beauty, as compared to theories of morality.

A modern thinker, J. Krishnamurti (2000) (p.125), delves on the question, in the following words:

"Sensitivity to beauty and to ugliness does not come about through attachment; it comes with love, when there are no self-created conflicts."

The development of a sense of discrimination between the beautiful and ugly is the most difficult task when we follow a set course. The indirect course is always the most effective that is taking the young minds on a voyage that captures their heart and slowly they begin to feel and experience beauty, not only physical but also absolute and mental. It exists in arts and crafts, objects of art created by men, literature using the medium of a language and also in natural scenes, mountains, falls, rise and setting of sun, moon and stars, rainbows, and not the least in mental abstractions like mathematics, geometry and philosophy. That is why Edna St. Vincent Millay wrote:

"Euclid alone has looked on beauty bare."

Apart from the use of figures of speech, appropriate words and verse forms, Vālmiki (*VR.*) sometimes depict nature through the medium of language tools as if constructing a landscape painting. Let's go to Pañcavaṭi with Rāma. The poet describes the scenic beauty of the place in the words of Rāma as follows:

iyamādityasaṅkāśaiḥ padmaiḥ surabhigandhibhiḥ
adūre dṛṣyate ramyā padmini padmaśobhita. (Āraṇya.15.11)

yathākhyātam Agastyen muninā bhavitātmanā
iyaṁ Godāvarī ramyā puṣpitais-tarubhirāvṛitā.
(Āraṇya.15.12)

Here is seen a lake looking delightful with fragrant sun-like lotuses and (further) beautified by blue lotuses. (11) As pointed out by Agastya, the pure-minded sage, this is the charming Godāvarī hemmed with trees in blossom. (12)

hansa-karanda-vakirṇa cakravākopśobhita
nātidūre na cāsanne mṛgayūthnipiḍita. (Āraṇya.15.13)

mayūrnadita ramyaḥ pranśavobāhukandaraḥ
dṛṣyante girayaḥ saumya fullaistaubhiravṛta. (Āraṇya.15.14)

Crowded with swans and Karandava birds, beautified by *Cakravāka* birds and stirred by herds of deer, it is neither very far nor very near. (13) here are seen lofty and charming mountains made noisy by peacocks, having many caves and covered with trees, in blossom, O gentle Lakṣmaṇa! (14)

After the abduction of Sitā by Rāvaṇa, Rāma proceeded to Kiṣkindhā to trace her. The natural beauty of the place through the eyes of a person whose most beloved partner has been lost, takes the shape of a marvellous description.

sa tāṁ puṣkariṇiṁ gatvā padmotpaljhaṣakulam
rāmaḥ saumitrasahito vilalāpākulendriyaā. (Kiṣkindhā.1.1)

Reaching along with Lakṣmaṇa, son of Sumitrā, the aforesaid pond abounding in lotuses, lilies, and fishes, Rāma, whose mind was troubled, burst into a wail. (1).

tatra dṛṣṭvaiva tāṁ harṣadindriyāṇi cākampire
sa kamvaśmapannaḥ saumitrimidamabravit. (Kiṣ.1.2)

saumitre shobhate pampā vaidūryavimlosaka
fullpadmotpalvati shobhita vividhairdrumaih. (Kiṣ.1.3)

saumitre paśya pampāyāḥ kananaṁ śubha-darśanam
Yatra rajanti shaila va drumah sashikhara iva. (Kiṣ.1.4)

Immediately on seeing the pond, the senses of Rāma felt excited. Fallen prey to love, he spoke as follows to Lakṣmaṇa: (2). Containing full-blown lotuses and lilies and adorned with trees of every description, and with its water transparent as a cat's-eye-gem, O Lakṣmaṇa, Pampā looks charming. (3) Behold, O Lakṣmaṇa, the woodland surrounding Pampā. So pleasant to the sight, the trees in which, looking as though crested, with their towering boughs, spread their charm like mountains (4). Further, it goes on

prastareṣu ca ramyeṣu vividhāḥ kānanadrumāḥ
vayuvegpracalitāḥ puṣpairavakiranti gām. (Kiṣ.1.12)

patitaiḥ patimanaiśca padapsthaiśca marutaḥ
kusumaiḥ paśya saumitre kṛḍatīva samantataḥ. (Kiṣ.1.13)

vikṣipan vividhāḥ śaka nagānām kusumotkaṭaḥ
marutaścalitasthanaiḥ khāṭpadairanugīyate. (Kiṣ.1.14)

Nay, shaken by the tempo of the blasts, forest trees of every description standing in the midst of pleasing flat rocks cover the ground with flowers (12). See how the breeze is sporting as it were on all sides with the flowers that have fallen, are falling, and are (still) on the trees, O Lakṣmaṇa, son of Sumitrā! (13) violently shaking the various branches, richly endowed with blossom, of trees, the breeze is being celebrated in song by black bees which have shifted from their position (on flowers, as they were dislodged by the breeze) (14).

In the world, there is some sort of beauty for every sense-organ and related sensation. Then, there are combinations of the experience from the senses, that, too, in every human field of action and interaction. Again, the sense of greater good has to be kept in mind as well as in the perspective. One must be reminded, that decency and decorum of behaviour and human inter-action always are within the premises of a sense of beauty. As such the ugliness must be deplored, be it harsh language, vulgar and obscene behaviour, ill-intentioned manipulations, or anything of similar nature. Sometimes minor evil is done, to avoid more bigger calamities. This happened when Vāli, the king of Vānaras (Mongols), was killed by Rāma, and his brother, who had been guilty of similar deeds was befriended. Rāma knew well that killing is bad, but in order to save the world from the greater evil, he chose the minor evil for him. The beauty of his killing-act is that he afterwards showed sincere affection towards his victims and exhibited no ill will towards them.

A Glimpse of Ethical Values in Manusmṛti

All *Smṛtis* must uphold the spirit of *Śruti.* Manu's *Manusmṛti* (MS), takes the foremost place, because his work is based on the teaching of the Veda. Manu's greatest contribution is his consideration of law as *dharma,* which etymologically means that which upholds or that which sustains. *Dharma,* the adherence to righteousness, is the very foundation of a just and sustainable society. Since humans have free will, they may choose not to adhere to *dharma* and then, the society will start regressing. In upholding *dharma,* man evolves towards perfection, in demeaning *dharma,* humanity sinks to sordid destruction. In this thought-provoking article, the learned author has cited many Vedic ethical values enshrined in *MS.* and still relevant in the modern times, which is facing the onslaught of degradation of moral values on all fronts. **- Editor**

prityajedarthakāmau yau syātāṁ dharmavarjitau.
dharmacāpyasukhodarka lokavikruṣṭameva ca.

(*Manu.* 4.176)

Reject wealth/money and desires which are contrary to *Dharma.* Reject also such rules of *Dharma* obedience to which lead to the unhappiness of a few or which cause public resentment.

Introduction

Manu, the great Indian sage, who is considered the oldest of lawmakers in the annals of human civilisation, has very beautifully given the essence of the Vedic Ethical Values, anointed as the cornerstone of the Indian philosophy. Manu occupies a dominant place in Indian thought; he is one of the legendary progenitors of the race, a patriarch embodying in himself the roles of both ruler and spiritual teacher. "*What Manu says is medicine*". The ordinances of Manu are considered to be as efficacious as the prescriptions of a physician *(Yad vai manur avadat tad bheṣajam).* If Pāṇini laid down the rules of Sanskrit grammar, then Manu laid down the rules of conduct for humanity at large for all times. However, we need to judge the *Manusmṛti* (*MS.*) in light of present times. In the words of Will Durant *'the historians' folly is to judge the past from the yardstick of the present'*, and we should accord *MS.* due to scholarly sensitivity, concern, and understanding. The 'Laws of Manu' or *'Manusmṛti'* or *Manu Saṁhitā* , the best-known ancient Indian treatise on religious law and social obligations, was probably first written down as per tradition at the beginning of the present 7th *Vaivasvata Manvantara.* Although commonly referred to as the "Laws" of Manu, **these are more moral precepts than actual legal statutes.**

Basically, the *Smṛtis* like *Manusmṛti,* are compilations of prescriptions and practices of various (mostly Vedic) schools and attempt to generalize rules of conduct for entire humanity during the epic and early classical periods. *The Smṛtis,* which are held to be an elaboration of the *Śrutis* or Vedas, are the principal codes of social law. The word '*smṛti*' means 'what is remembered' and is generally applied to all authoritative texts other than the Vedas. Thus, the *Smṛtis* are a sort of general guide books to social living under different circumstances and at different times. They supplement and explain the sociological and ritualistic injunctions of the Vedas, called *Vidhi,* and are thus called *Dharma-Śāstras* (scriptures on *Dharma*). Among the *Smṛtis,* the *Smṛtis* of Manu, Yājñavalkya and Pārāśara are the most authoritative and renowned.

According to Manu, *Dharma* is to be known through the Vedas, *Smṛtis,* the conduct of saints, who know and practise this *Dharma,* and finally one's own purified conscience. **By following *Dharma,* one attains perfection.** It is *Dharma* alone that comes to one's aid in the end. The *MS.* is regarded as the oldest codification of rules of *Dharma,* which is a comprehensive term for all rules of righteous conduct in every sphere of human activities. The *MS.* lays down the laws which regulate national, communal, family, and individual obligations in general (*Sāmānya*) as well as in particular (*Viśeṣa*), specializing in details on the *Dharmas* (duties) pertaining to the four *Varṇas* (four personality types of people in society), viz., *Brāhmaṇas* or those who are by nature philosophers and spiritualists, *Kṣatriyas*, those who are by nature fighters, *Vaiśyas* or those who are by nature businessmen, and *Śudras* or who are by nature labourers or producers. The Smṛti also deals with the *Dharma* of *Brahmacārins* or students leading a life of continence and study under a preceptor or *Guru, Gṛhasthas* or householders who form the active, functional and professional aspect of the society, *Vānaprasthas* or recluses and hermits who have retired from active life as a preparation for the pursuit of spiritual realisation, and *Sannyasins* or monks who have renounced the world of activity and social contact for complete dedication to the ideal of the realisation of the Absolute. Summing up his instructions, he says that, of all *Dharmas,* **the knowledge of the Self is supreme,** for thereby one attains immortality. By seeing the Self in all beings and all beings in the Self, and practising thus equality of vision, one attains absolute suzerainty or Self-realisation. The essence of *Dharma* consists in the practice of fortitude (*Dhṛti),* forbearance (*Kṣ amā*), sense-control (*Dāma),* non-appropriation of what does not belong to oneself (*Asteya*), purity in thought, word and deed (*Śauca*), restraint of mind (*Indriyanigraha),* clarified understanding (*Dhī*), knowledge of Truth (Vidyā), truthfulness (*Satya*) and freedom from anger (*Akrodha*) (*MS.* 6.92).

The *Manusmṛti* (MS.), which is the Manual on ***dharma*** **(right behaviour, law, morality and such things)** has **2,694 stanzas in 12 chapters.** MS. deals with interesting cosmogony, ***definitions of what is right and fit (dharma)***, the sacraments, initiation and Vedic study, forms of marriage, hospitality and other rites, dietary laws, pollution and purification, rules for women and wives, royal law, many sorts of juridical matters, and also more religious matters, which include donations, rites, the doctrine of *karma* ("giving-back"), the soul, and punishment, etc. Thus, the law in the juridical sense is embedded in old religious law and practice. The framework for the notions and rules meted out is the ancient model of a four-class society. The influence of the *Dharmaśāstra* (Law Book) of Manu has been enormous, as it provided Hindu society with its practical morality. Let us have a glimpse of the Vedic ethical and moral values and the code of conduct prescribed in the *Manusmṛti*, to adjudge how many of the moral concepts are still valid even in the present times, when the deterioration of moral standards is shattering the very moral fabric of the society at large.

(A) Source of Manusmṛti

The whole Veda (*Śruti*) is the (first) source of the sacred law, next to the tradition and the virtuous conduct of those who know the Veda, also the customs of holy men, and (finally) self-satisfaction. The Veda, the sacred tradition, the customs of virtuous men, and one's own pleasure, they declare to be visibly the fourfold means of defining the sacred law. By *Śruti* (revelation) is meant the Veda, and by *Smṛti* (tradition) the Institutes of the sacred law. The custom handed down in regular succession (since time immemorial) among the (four chief *varṇas)* and the mixed (races) of that country (India), is called the conduct of virtuous men (*MS.* 2.18). But a learned man after fully scrutinising all this with the eye of knowledge, should, in accordance with the authority of the revealed texts, be intent on (the performance of) his duties (*MS.* 2.8). According to the *Manusmṛti*, by the study of the Veda, by vows, by burnt oblations, by (the recitation of) sacred texts, by the (acquisition of the) threefold sacred science, by offering (to the gods, Rishis, and manes), by (the procreation of) sons, by the great *yajñas*, and by (*Śrauta*) rites, this (human) body is made fit for (union with) Brahman (2.28).

(B) Knowledge of the Vedas

1. An Aryan (*śreṣṭha* or excellent person) must study the whole Veda together with the *Rahasyas,* performing at the same time various kinds of austerities and the vows prescribed by the rules (of the Veda) (2.165).

2. Unless one is asked, one must not explain (anything) to anybody, nor (must one answer) a person who asks improperly; let a wise man, though he knows (the

answer), behave among men as (if he were) an idiot (2.110).

3. Where merit and wealth are not (obtained by teaching) nor (at least) due obedience, in such (soil) sacred knowledge must not be sown, just as good seed (must) not (be thrown) on barren land (2.112). Even in times of dire distress, a teacher of the Veda should rather die with his knowledge than sow it in barren soil (2.113).
4. Of him who gives natural birth and him who gives (the knowledge) the Veda, the giver of the Veda is the more venerable father; for the birth for the sake of the Veda (ensures) eternal (rewards) both in this (life) and after death (2.146).
5. By daily reciting the Veda, by (the observance of the rules of) purification, by (practising) austerities, and by doing no injury to created beings, one (obtains the faculty of) remembering former births (*MS.* 4.148).
6. Neither through years, nor through white (hairs), nor through wealth, nor through (powerful) kinsmen (comes greatness). The sages have made this law, 'He who has learnt the Veda together with the *Aṅgas* is (considered) great by us' (2.154). A man is not, therefore (considered) venerable because his head is gray; him who, though young, has learnt the Veda, the gods consider to be venerable (2.156).
7. The eternal lore of the **Veda** upholds all created beings; hence I (Manu) hold that to be **supreme**, which is the means of (securing happiness to) these creatures (*MS.*12.99).
8. The Veda is the eternal eye of the manes, gods, and men; the Veda-ordinance (is) both beyond the sphere of (human) power, and beyond the sphere of (human) comprehension; that is a certain fact (*MS.*12.94).
9. All those traditions (*smṛti*) and those despicable systems of philosophy, which are not based on the Veda, produce no reward after death; for they are

declared to be founded on Darkness (*MS.*12.95).

10. The four Varṇas, the three worlds, the four orders, the past, the present, and the future are all severally known by means of the Veda (*MS.*12.97).

11. Sound, touch, colour, taste, and fifthly smell are known through the **Veda** alone, (their) production (is) through the (Vedic rites, which in this respect are) secondary acts. (*MS.* 12.98).

12. As a fire that has gained strength consumes even trees full of sap, even so, he who knows the **Veda** burns out the taint of his soul which arises from (evil) acts (*MS.*12.101).

13. In whatever order (a man) who knows the true meaning of the **Vedic-science** may dwell, he becomes even while abiding in this world, fit for the union with Brahman (*MS.* 12.102).

(C) Recitation of 'Om' and *Sāvitrī*

1. Let him (the student) always pronounce the syllable **Om** at the beginning and at the end of (a lesson in) the Veda; (for) unless the syllable **Om** precede (the lesson) will slip away (from him), and unless it follows it will fade away (2.74).

2. *Prajāpati* (the lord of creatures) milked out (as it were) from the three Vedas the sounds A, U, and M, and (the *Vyāhṛtis*) *Bhūḥ, Bhuvaḥ, Svaḥ* (2.76); He milked out from the three Vedas (as it were) that *Ṛk* - verse, sacred to *Sāvitrī* (2.77).

3. Let him stand during the morning twilight, muttering the *Sāvitri* until the sun appears, but (let him recite it), seated, in the evening until the constellations can be seen distinctly (2.101). He who stands during the morning twilight muttering (the *Sāvitrī*), removes the guilt concentrated during the (previous) night; but he who (recites it), seated, in the evening, destroys the sin he committed during the day (2.102). But he who does

not (worship) standing in the morning, nor sitting in the evening, shall be excluded from all the duties and rights of an Aryan (2.103).

(D) Allurement to Sensual Pleasures

1. A wise man should strive to restrain his organs which run wild among alluring sensual objects, like a charioteer his horses (*MS.* 2.88). Know that the internal organ (*manas*) has been subdued, both those (two) sets of five (external organs) have been conquered (*MS.* 2.92). Through the attachment of his organs (to sensual pleasure) a man doubtlessly will incur guilt; but if he keeps them under complete control, he will obtain success (in gaining all his aims) (2.93.)
2. Desire is never extinguished by the enjoyment of desired objects; it only grows stronger like a fire (fed) with clarified butter (2.94). If one man should obtain all those (sensual enjoyments) and another should renounce them all, the renunciation of all pleasure is far better than the attainment of them. (2.95)
3. Those (organs) which are strongly attached to sensual pleasures, cannot so effectually be restrained by abstinence (from enjoyments) as by a *constant (pursuit of true) knowledge* (2.96). Neither (the study of) the Vedas, nor liberality, nor *yajñas*, nor any (self-imposed) restraint, nor austerities, ever procure the attainment (of rewards) to a man whose heart is contaminated (by sensuality) (2.97). If he keeps all the (ten) organs as well as the mind in subjection, he may gain all his aims, without reducing his body by (the practice) of *Yoga* (2.100). But when one among all the organs slips away (from control), thereby (man's) wisdom slips away from him, even as the water (flows) through the one (open) foot of a (water-carrier's) skin (2.99).
4. He who desires happiness must strive after a perfectly *contented disposition* and control himself; for *happiness*

has contentment for its root, the root of unhappiness is the contrary (disposition) (*MS.* 4.12). Let him not, out of desire (for enjoyments), attach himself to any sensual pleasures, and let him carefully obviate an excessive attachment to them, by (reflecting on their worthlessness in) his heart (*MS.* 4.16).

5. That man may be considered to have (really) subdued his organs, who on hearing and touching and seeing, on tasting and smelling (anything) *neither rejoices nor repines* (*MS.* 2.98).

6. In consequence of attachment to (the objects of) the senses, and in consequence of the non-performance of their duties, fools, the lowest of men, reach the vilest births (*MS.* 12.52).

7. Coveting the property of others, thinking in one's heart of what is undesirable, and adherence to false (doctrines), are the *three kinds of (sinful) mental actions* (12.5).

8. Abusing (others, speaking) untruth, detracting from the merits of all men, and talking idly, shall be the *four kinds of (evil) verbal action* (*MS.* 12.6). Taking what has not been given, injuring (creatures) without the sanction of the law, and holding criminal intercourse with another man's wife, are declared to be the *three kinds of (wicked) bodily actions* (*MS.* 12.7).

9. (A man) obtains (the result of) a good or evil mental (act) in his mind, (that of) a verbal (act) in his speech, (that of) a bodily (act) in his body (*MS.* 12.8).

(E) Respect to Elders

1. He who habitually salutes and constantly pays reverence to the aged obtains an increase of four (things), (viz.) length of life, knowledge, fame, (and) strength (*MS.* 2.121)

2. One must not sit down on a couch or seat which a superior occupies; and he who occupies a couch or seat

shall rise to meet a (superior), and (afterwards) salute him. For the vital airs of a young man mount upwards to leave his body when an elder approaches; but by rising to meet him and saluting he recovers them (*MS.* 2.119-120).

3. Way must be made for a man in a carriage, for one who is above ninety years old, for one diseased, for the carrier of a burden, for a woman, for a *Snātaka*, for the king, and for a bridegroom (*MS.* 2.138).

4. Wealth, kindred, age, (the due performance of) rites, and, fifthly, *sacred learning* are titles to respect; but each later-named (cause) is more weighty (than the preceding ones) (*MS.* 2.136).

(F) Dietary Rules of Conduct

1. Let a twice-born man **always eat his food with a concentrated mind**, after performing an ablution (2.53)

2. Let him always worship his food, and eat it without contempt; when he sees it, let him rejoice, show a pleased face, and pray that he may always obtain it. (2.54). Food, that is always worshipped, gives strength and manly vigour; but eaten irreverently, it destroys them both (2.55).

3. Let him not give to any man what he leaves, and beware of eating between (the two meal-times); let him not over-eat himself, nor go anywhere without having purified himself (after his meal) (2.56).

4. *Excessive eating is prejudicial to health, to fame, and to (bliss in) heaven*; it prevents (the acquisition of) spiritual merit, and is odious among men; one ought, for these reasons, to avoid it carefully (2.57).

5. He who prepares food for himself (alone), eats nothing but sin; for it is ordained that the food which remains after (the performance of) the yajñas shall be the meal of virtuous men (*MS.* 3.118).

(G) Gentle Speech

1. Created beings must be instructed in (what concerns) their welfare without giving them pain, and sweet and gentle speech must be used by (a teacher) who desires (to abide by) the sacred law (2.159).

2. He, forsooth, whose speech and thoughts are pure and ever perfectly guarded, gains the whole reward which is conferred by the Veda (2.160).

3. Let him not, even though in pain, (speak words) cutting (others) to the quick; let him not injure others in thought or deed; let him not utter speeches which make (others) afraid of him, since that will prevent him from gaining heaven (2.161).

4. A learned visionary man should always fear homage as if it were poison; and constantly desire (to suffer) scorn as (he would long for) nectar (2.162). For he who is scorned (nevertheless may) sleep with an easy mind, awake with an easy mind, and with an easy mind walk here among men; but the scorner utterly perishes (2.163).

5. Let him say what is true, let him say what is pleasing, let him utter no disagreeable truth, and let him utter no agreeable falsehood; that is the eternal law (*MS.* 4.138).

6. All things (have their nature) determined by speech; speech is their root, and from speech, they proceed; but he who is dishonest with respect to speech, is dishonest in everything (*MS.* 4.256).

(H) Code of Conduct and Ethical Values

Manusmṛti expounds the Code of Conduct and Ethical Values *inter alia* in the following verses:

Sattva, Rajas, and *Tamas* Qualities (*Guṇas*) :

1. Know *sattva*, *rajas*, and *tamas* to be the three qualities of the Self, with which the Great One always

completely pervades all existence (*MS.* 12.24). When one of these qualities wholly predominates in a body, then it makes the embodied (soul) eminently distinguished for that quality (*MS.* 12.25).

2. *Sattva* (Goodness) is declared (to have the form of) knowledge, *Tamas* (Darkness) (of) ignorance, *Rajas* (Activity) (of) love and hatred; such is the nature of these (three) which is (all-) pervading and clings to everything created (*MS.* 12.26).

3. When (man) experiences in his soul a (feeling) full of bliss, a deep calm, as it were, and a pure light, then let him know (that it is) among those three (the quality called) *Sattva* (*MS.* 12.27).

4. What is mixed with pain and does not give satisfaction to the soul one may know (to be the quality of) *Rajas*, which is difficult to conquer, and whichever draws embodied (souls towards sensual objects) (*MS.*12.28). What is coupled with delusion, what has the character of an indiscernible mass, what cannot be fathomed by reasoning, what cannot be fully known, one must consider (as the quality of) *Tamas* (*MS.* 12. 29).

5. The study of the Vedas, austerity, (the pursuit of) knowledge, purity, control over the organs, the performance of meritorious acts and meditation on the Soul, (are) the marks of the quality of *Sattva* (*MS.* 12.31). Delighting in undertakings, want of firmness, commission of sinful acts, and continual indulgence in sensual pleasures, (are) the marks of the quality of *Rajas* (*MS.* 12.32). Covetousness, sleepiness, pusillanimity, cruelty, atheism, leading an evil life, a habit of soliciting favours, and inattentiveness, are the marks of the quality of *Tamas* (*MS.* 12.33). When a (man), having done, doing, or being about to do any act, feels ashamed, the learned may know that all (such acts bear) the mark of the quality of *Tamas* (*MS.* 12.35). But, when (a man) desires (to gain) by an act much fame in this world and feels no sorrow on failing,

know that it (bears the mark of the quality of) *Rajas* (*MS.* 12.36).

6. But that (bears) the mark of the quality of *Sattva* which with his whole (heart) he desires to know, which he is not ashamed to perform, and at which his soul rejoices.

7. The craving after sensual pleasures is declared to be the mark of *Tamas*, (the pursuit of) wealth (the mark) of *Rajas*, (the desire to gain) spiritual merit the mark of *Sattva*; each later named quality is better than the preceding one (*MS.* 12.38).

Code of Conduct in General

1. He who possesses faith may receive pure learning even from a man of lower *varṇa*, the highest law even from the lowest, and an excellent wife even from a base family (2.238). Excellent wives, learning, (the knowledge of) the law, (the rules of) purity, good advice, and various arts may be acquired from anybody (2.240). Even from poison, nectar may be taken, even from a child good advice, even from a foe (a lesson in) good conduct, and even from an impure (substance) gold (2.239).

2. Wealth, kindred, age, (the due performance of) rites, and, fifthly, sacred learning are titles to respect; but each later-named (cause) is more weighty (than the preceding ones) (2.136).

3. As the man who digs with a spade (into the ground) obtains water, even so, an obedient (pupil) obtains the knowledge which lies (hidden) in his teacher (2.218).

4. The seniority of *Brahmaṇas* is from (sacred) knowledge, that of *Kṣatriyas* from valour, that of *Vaiśyas* from wealth in grain (and other goods), but that of *Śudras* alone from age (2.155). As an elephant made of wood, as an antelope made of leather, such is an unlearned *Brāhmaṇa*; those three have nothing but the names (of their kind) (2.157). As a eunuch is unproductive with women, as a cow with a cow is

unproductive, and as a gift made to an ignorant man yields no reward, even so, is a *Brāhmaṇa* useless, who (does) not (know) the *Riks* (2.158).

5. Whatever is dependent on others is misery; whatever rests on oneself is happiness; this in brief is the definition of happiness and misery. (4.160). Let him carefully avoid all undertakings (the success of) which depends on others; but let him eagerly pursue that (the accomplishment of) which depends on himself (*MS.* 4.159).
6. One should not allow one's spirit to be frustrated by earlier failures; till death one should strive for prosperity and should never consider it difficult to attain (*MS.* 4.137).
7. When the performance of an act gladdens his heart, let him perform it with diligence; but let him avoid the opposite (*MS.* 4.161).
8. No calamity happens to those who eagerly follow auspicious customs and the rule of good conduct, to those who are always careful of purity, and to those who mutter (sacred texts) and offer burnt-oblations (*MS.* 4.146).
9. Neither a man who (lives) unrighteously, nor he who (acquires) wealth (by telling) falsehoods, nor he who always delights in doing injury, ever attain happiness in this world (*MS.* 4.170).
10. Let him avoid (the acquisition of) wealth and (the gratification of his) desires, if they are opposed to the Dharma (the sacred law), and even lawful acts which may cause pain in the future or are offensive to men (*MS.* 4.176).
11. Giving no pain to any creature, let him slowly accumulate spiritual merit, for the sake (of acquiring) a companion to the next world, just as the white ant (gradually raises its) hill. For in the next world neither father, nor mother, nor wife, nor sons, nor relations

stays to be his companions; spiritual merit alone remains (with him). Single is each being born; single it dies; single it enjoys (the reward of its) virtue; single (it suffers the punishment of its) sin (*MS.* 4.238-40). He who is persevering, gentle, (and) patient, shuns the company of men of cruel conduct, and does no injury (to living creatures), gains, if he constantly lives in that manner, by controlling his organs and by liberality, heavenly bliss (*MS.* 4.246).

12. He who injures innoxious beings from a wish to (give) himself pleasure, never finds happiness, neither living nor dead (*MS.* 5.45). He who does not seek to cause the sufferings of bonds and death to living creatures, (but) desires the good of all (beings), obtains endless bliss (*MS.* 5.46). He who does not injure any (creature), attains without an effort what he thinks of, what he undertakes, and what he fixes his mind on (*MS.* 5.47).

13. Meat can never be obtained without injury to living creatures, and injury to sentient beings is detrimental to (the attainment of) heavenly bliss; let him, therefore, shun (the use of) meat (*MS.* 5.48). Having well considered the (disgusting) origin of flesh and the (cruelty of) fettering and slaying corporeal beings, let him entirely abstain from eating flesh (*MS.* 5.49).

14. Among all modes of purification, purity in (the acquisition of) wealth is declared to be the best; for he is pure who gains wealth with clean hands (*MS.* 5.106). The body is cleansed by water, the internal organ is purified by truthfulness, the individual soul by sacred learning and austerities, the intellect by (true) knowledge (*MS.* 5.109).

15. Contentment, forgiveness, self-control, abstention from unrighteously appropriating anything, (obedience to the rules of) purification, coercion of the organs, wisdom, knowledge (of the supreme Soul), truthfulness, and abstention from anger, (form) the tenfold law (*MS.*

6.92).

16. And in accordance with the precepts of the Veda and of the *Smṛti, the Gṛhastha* (householder) is declared to be superior to all of them; for he supports the other three. As all rivers, both great and small, find a resting-place in the ocean, even so, men of all orders find protection with householders (*MS.* 6.89-90).

17. *Dharma* (values), being discarded, destroys; *Dharma*, being preserved, preserves: therefore, *Dharma* must not be discarded, lest discarded *Dharma* destroys us (*MS.* 8.15). For divine *Dharma* (is said to be) a bull (*vṛṣa*); that (man) who violates it (*kurute'lam*) the gods consider to be (a man despicable like) a *Śudra* (*vṛṣala*); let him, therefore, beware of discarding *Dharma* (*MS.* 8.16).

18. The only friend who follows men even after death is *Dharma*; for everything else is lost at the same time when the body perishes (*MS.* 8.17).

19. But with whatever disposition of mind (a man) forms any act, he reaps its result in a (future) body endowed with the same quality (*MS.* 12.81).

20. Studying the Veda, (practising) austerities, (the acquisition of true) knowledge, the subjugation of the organs, abstention from doing injury, and serving the Guru are the best means for attaining supreme bliss (*MS.* 12.83). (If you ask) whether among all these virtuous actions, (performed) here below, (there be) one which has been declared more efficacious (than the rest) for securing supreme happiness to man (*MS.* 12.84) (The answer is that) the knowledge of the Soul is stated to be the most excellent among all of them; for that is the first of all sciences, because immortality is gained through that (*MS.* 12.85).

21. He who sacrifices to the Self (alone), equally recognising the Self in all created beings and all created beings in the Self, becomes (independent like) an

autocrat and self-luminous (*MS.*12.91). Let him, concentrating his mind, fully recognise in the Self all things, both the real and the unreal, for he who recognises the universe in the Self, does not give his heart to unrighteousness (*MS.* 12.118). The Self alone is the multitude of the gods, the universe rests on the Self; for the Self produces the connection of these embodied (spirits) with actions (*MS.* 12.119). He who thus recognises the Self through the Self in all created beings, becomes equal (minded) towards all, and enters the highest state, *Brahman* (*MS.* 12.125).

22. Manu declares 'non-violence, constant adherence to truth, non-thieving, being pure, and keeping the senses in control- this is the essentially common *dharma* for all the four *Varṇas*' (*MS.* 10.62).

Manu (*MS.* 12.35) has given the essence of the ethical values in the following verse:

1. If a man in his conscience, feels ashamed/guilty to do an act, or while doing an act, or after doing an act, it is the clearest indication of *Tamasa* Quality -viz, the act is a sin.
2. Thus, the soul *(Ātma)* constantly reminds a person of his/her misdemeanours. It is for this reason that the individual feels ashamed within, though before others he may try to pose as a good man. It calls upon every individual to establish an internal check, which alone is the guarantee for good conduct, as if he listens to his conscience he will not commit the sin.

Manu (*MS.* 8.84) rouses the conscience of an individual in a verse which is intended to be part of an exhortation to witness:

1. The Soul itself is the witness of the Soul and the Soul is the refuge of the soul despise not thy own Soul the supreme witness to the acts of men'.

2. One should not be under the impression that one can do wrong or evil in secret, without the knowledge of others, for

the very sky, earth, water, sun, moon, fire, wind, day and night, and one's own heart and soul, will stand witness to one's action in due course of time.' Restraining one's mind in a state of equilibrium of thought, one should visualise both the good and the bad as appearances of the Self, to put an end to all inclination to unrighteousness. The Self alone is all, the gods and everything is contained in the Self. That is to be known as the Supreme *Puruṣa* which is the ordainer of all things, subtler than the subtle and realisable by sharp understanding. The eternal advise by Manu for all human beings to be followed throughout life is: not to indulge in self- deception. The soul is the witness, the soul is the police, the soul is the judge. The soul is capable of indicating what is wrong and what is right. A man with good *saṁskāra* immediately yields to the advice. But a man who is unable to control his desire, falls prey to the sinful desire. This is the fate of those who commit murder, rape, who indulge in corruption and who are ultimately caught and punished. They may not be caught, or even if caught and prosecuted for want of evidence in the courts, they may not go to jail, but they are bound to suffer by losing mental peace and by loss of reputation for themselves and members of their families. That is why, it is said that death is preferable to the loss of reputation.'

Manu (*MS*: 4.174) again warns every individual in the following words:

> 'Those who indulge in *adharma* (may) attain immediate success and secure fulfillment of their desires. They overpower their opponents. But ultimately their ruin down to the roots is certain.'

Human Desires

> 'There is no act of man which is free from desire; whatever a man does is the result of the impulse of desire' (*MS.* 2.4).

Manu states that the force behind every action of a human being is his desire (*kāma).* The natural desire of man was found to be the desire to have the enjoyment of wealth i.e., material pleasure (*artha*) as also emotional and sexual enjoyment (*kāma*), culminating in all evil actions of human beings, which in turn gave rise to a conflict of interests among individuals. Further, it was found that the desire (*kāma*) of human beings could also be influenced by the other impulses inherent in human beings such as anger (*krodha*), passion (*moha*), greed (*lobha),* infatuation (*mada*), and enmity (*mātsarya*). These six natural impulses were considered as six internal enemies of man (*ari-ṣaḍvarga*), which if allowed to act uncontrolled could instigate him to entertain evil thoughts in the mind for fulfilling his own selfish desires and for that purpose cause injury to others. Manu, on this basis, explained the causes of all civil and criminal injuries inflicted by the action of one against the other.

1. To act solely from a desire for rewards is not laudable. The desire (for rewards), indeed, has its root in the conception that an act can yield them, and in consequence of (that) conception sacrifices are performed; vows and the laws prescribing restraints are all stated to be kept through the idea that they will bear fruit, for whatever (man) does, it is (the result of) the impulse of desire (*MS.* 2.2-3).

The consequences of not controlling desires which arise in the mind are explained in the *Bhagvadgītā* (Ch. II, 62-63).

> 'When a man begins to think of securing anything in the first instance attachment to that develops. Attachment leads to desire; when the desire is not fulfilled it leads to anger; anger, in turn, leads to lose of sense of good and bad; this loss leads to destruction of sound discretion and finally; the loss of sound discretion leads to total destruction -the man perishes.'

How true it is! We see everyday the human beings just to achieve their selfish purposes indulging in all sorts of crimes, misappropriation, the onslaught on women, corruption. This ultimately ruins them and their families and also adversely affects society as a whole.

Dharma

Mahābhārata the great epic which is acclaimed as the *Mānava Kartavya Śāstra* (code of duties of human beings) contains a discussion of this topic. On being asked by Yudhiṣṭ hira to explain the meaning and scope of *Dharma,* Bhīṣma who had mastered the knowledge of *Dharma* replied thus:

तादृशोऽयमनुप्रश्नो यत्र धर्मः सुदुर्लभः।
दुष्करः प्रतिसंख्यातुं तत्केनात्र व्यवस्यति।।

प्रभवार्थाय भूतानां धर्मप्रवचनं कृतम्।
स स्यात्प्रभवसंयूक्तः स धर्म इति निश्चयः।। *Śāntiparva*- 109.9.11

> It is most difficult to define *Dharma*. *Dharma* has been explained to be that which helps the upliftment of living beings. Therefore, that which ensures the welfare of living beings is surely *Dharma*. The learned rishis have declared that which sustains universal life is *Dharma*.

Again in *Karṇa Parva* (of the *Mahābhārata*) eulogises *Dharma* in the following words:

> *Dharma* sustains the society, *Dharma* maintains the social order, *Dharma* ensures the well-being and progress of Humanity. *Dharma* is surely that which fulfils these objectives. (Ch. 69 Verse 58)

Manusmṛti has brought '*Dharma*' under five heads:

> '*Ahiṁsā* (non-violence), *Satya* (truthfulness), *Asteya* (not acquiring illegitimate wealth), *Śaucam* (purity), and *Indriyanigraha* (control of senses) are, in brief, the common *Dharma* for all the *varṇas*'.

Thus, Abstention from injuring (creatures), veracity, abstention from unlawfully appropriating (the goods of others), purity, and control of the organs, Manu has declared to be the summary of the law for the four castes. According to Justice Rama M. Jois, 'The *first rule* is not to indulge in violence against other living beings. *The second* rule requires every one to be *truthful* in day to day life. *The third* rule 'of not acquiring illegitimate wealth' is of the utmost importance. It is the desire to secure wealth by illegal methods which makes a man corrupt, a cheat, a smuggler, a black marketeer, an exploiter, and makes even men in noble professions exploit the miseries of others to make more and more money in utter disregard to professional ethics. Therefore, it is very essential to ingrain in the heart and mind of every individual the desire not to indulge in *'asteya'* i.e., acquiring wealth by illegitimate and immoral methods. The *fourth* one commands every individual to maintain purity of thought, word and deed (*Trikaraṇa śuddhi* i.e., *Kāyā, Vācā, Manasā*), which is also called *Antaraṅga Śuddhi* (internal/mental purity) and *Bahiraṅga Śuddhi* (external purity or purity in action). This rule means absolute honesty in that there should be harmony in thought, word and deed of an individual. One should not think something in the mind, speak something else, and do entirely another thing. *The fifth* rule i.e., control of senses is also important, as it is lack of control over the senses which results in individuals indulging in all types of illegal and immoral actions, being instigated by the one or more of the six inherent enemies (*Ari-ṣaḍvargas*). This lands himself as well as others in misery and loss of happiness.' However, the mere knowledge of the rules of *Dharma* does not make a man *'Dharmiṣṭha'* i.e., a man acting always in conformity with *Dharma*. Therefore, *Dharma* has to be ingrained in the mind of every individual from child hood. According to Justice M. Rama Jois, '*just as triple antigen for giving immunity to the body against dreaded disease has to be administered to a young child for giving immunity to the mind against sinful thoughts Dharma- the sextuple antigen has to be administered to the mind of an individual as part of education. It is a slow but a sure process. This process was called 'Sanskāra'.*

While *Dharma* touches on a wide varieties of topics, the essence of *Dharma* common to all human beings has also been declared in *Mahābhārata*:

> *akrodhaḥ satyavachanaṁ saṁvibhāgaḥ kṣamā tathā*
> *prajanaḥ sveṣu dāreṣu śaicham-adroha eva ca*
> *ārjavaṁ bhṛtyabharaṇaṁ navaite sārvavarṇikḥ*
>
> *Mahābhārata* (*Śānti Parva* : 60.7.8)

"Being free from anger, (*Akrodaḥ*) sharing one's wealth with others, (*Saṁvibhāgaḥ*) forgiveness, (*Kṣamā*) truthfulness, procreation of children from ones wife alone, purity (in mind, thought and deed), (*Śaucam*) not betraying the trust or confidence reposed, (*Adrohaḥ*) absence of enmity, maintaining the persons dependent on oneself, these are the nine rules of Dharma to be followed by persons belonging to all sections of society".

'Truthfulness, to be free from anger, sharing wealth with others, (*saṁvibhāga*) forgiveness, procreation of children from one's wife alone, purity, absence of enmity, straightforwardness and maintaining persons dependent on oneself are the nine rules of the *Dharma* of persons belonging to all the *varṇas*'.

Rejection of *Artha* and *Kāma* if against *Dharma* :

parityajedarthakāmau yau syātāṁ dharmavarjitau.
Dharma chāpyasukhodarka lokavikruṣṭameva ca.
(*MS.* 4.176)

'Reject wealth/money and desires which are contrary to *Dharma.* Reject also such rules of *Dharma* obedience which lead to unhappiness of a few or which cause public resentment.'

It means that *Dharma* must control the desire *(kāma)* as well as the means of acquisition of wealth and deriving pleasure *(artha)*. *Dharma,* therefore, prescribes the rules of right conduct, observance of which was considered necessary for the welfare of the individual and society. Considering an integrated view of life, rules of right conduct covering almost every sphere of human activity such as religion, rules regulating personal conduct of an individual, as a student, as a teacher, as a house-holder, as a husband, as a wife, as a son, as a hermit, as an ascetic, including rules regulating taking of food and the like were prescribed in *MS. Dharma* therefore laid down a code of conduct covering every aspect of human behaviour, the observance of which was considered a must for the peace and happiness of individuals and society.

The principles set out above are fundamental and have manifested themselves through various provisions meant to sustain the life of the individual and society. It is for this reason, all the works on *Dharma* declare with one voice that *Dharma* is that which sustains the world. Every act or conduct which was in disobedience to rules of *Dharma* was called *Adharma* and was declared to be injurious to society and the individual.

Observance of Dharma a Must for Peaceful Co-

existence

The necessity of scrupulous practice of *Dharma* is forcefully expressed by Manu (8.15)

Dharma eva hato hanta dharmo rakṣati rakṣitaḥ
tasmāddhramo na hantavyo mā no dharmo'hato'vadhīt.

Dharma (Values) protects those who protect it. Those who destroy *Dharma* get destroyed. Therefore, *Dharma* should not be destroyed so that we may not be destroyed as a consequence thereof.

According to Justice M. Rama Jois, 'The principle laid down in this saying is of the utmost importance and significance. In the above very short saying, the entire concept of Rule of Law is incorporated. The meaning it conveys is that an orderly society would be in existence if everyone acts according to *Dharma* and thereby protect *Dharma*, and such an orderly society which would be an incarnation of *Dharma*, in turn, protects the rights of individuals. Rules of *Dharma* were meant to regulate the individual conduct, in such a way as to restrict the rights, liberty, interest and desires of an individual as regards all matters to the extent necessary in the interest of other individuals, i.e., society and at the same time making it obligatory for society to safeguard and protect an individual in all respects through its social and political institutions. Briefly put, *Dharma* regulated the mutual obligations of the individual and society. Therefore, it was stressed that the protection of *Dharma* was in the interest of both the individual and society. *Manusmṛti* warns: Do not destroy *Dharma*, so that you may not be destroyed. A 'State of *Dharma*' was required to be always maintained for peaceful co-existence, happiness and prosperity.' It is needless to state that it is only when a substantial number of citizens of a nation are by and large of "*Dharma* / law-abiding Nature" the Rule of law can be maintained. But, if the majority are not of a law-abiding nature, the nation gets destroyed.'

Values of Life

The *Manusmṛti* has laid down a system of values of life

which welded the people of India into a nation and all these values come within the purview of *Dharma*. It prescribed 'Duty Towards Others' including *Sāmānya Dharma* -A Code of Conduct for all human beings, *Rāja Dharma* -The Duty of Rulers, Respect for Womanhood, Equality (*Samānatā*), Gratitude (*Kṛtajñatā*), Compassion (*Dayā),* Simple Life - Sparing use of Natural Resources, Service (*Sevā-Paropakāra*), Sacrifice (*Tyāga).*

Duty towards other living beings

In Vedic culture and civilization, primary importance attached was to duty-based society, in which the right given to an individual was the right to perform his duty. This position is declared in the following verse of the Bhagavadgita thus:

karmaṇyevādhikārste

Your right (adhikāra) is to perform your duty.

Neither should one cling to life nor court death, but live a life of non-attachment, doing one's duty properly. This duty-based philosophy laid down for the individual and society makes India qualitatively different from others. This is a need-based culture in contrast to greed-based civilizations. The right given to an individual is the right to perform his duty. It is this philosophy which is the essence of the Vedic Culture. This value alone can instil in individuals the desire to perform their duty and to surrender/sacrifice their personal interests in the larger interest of the nation and/or humanity.

Causes for evil actions: *MS.* (12.3-7) analyses causes for evil action as follows:

'Action which springs from the mind, from speech and from the body produces either good or evil results. By action are caused various conditions of men. The mind is the instigator for all actions which are connected with and performed by the body. They are of three kinds and fall under ten heads:

Three sinful mental actions: A sin takes its origin in the mind in three ways:

- Coveting the property of others;

- Thinking what is undesirable; and
- Adherence to evil doctrines.

These three types of sinful mental actions give rise to four types of evil verbal actions or three types of wicked bodily actions:

The four evil verbal actions:

- Speaking an untruth;
- Attacking another in abusive or strong language
- Carrying tales against another person; and
- ज्ंसापदह पसस व िवजीमतेण

The three wicked bodily actions are:

- Taking what is not given;
- Injuring living beings and
- Illicit intercourse with another man's wife

According to Justice M. Rama Jois, 'the aforesaid analysis of the various evil mental and bodily actions cover the whole field of civil or criminal injury that an individual causes to another. The instigation comes from the mind. Thus, the sin first takes root in the form of mental action and thereafter expresses itself in the form of verbal or bodily evil actions which inflict civil or criminal injury as the case may be on others against whom they are directed. All the civil and criminal injuries which an individual may cause to others, such as appropriating the property belonging to others or denying what is due to others, or defamation, assault, theft, cheating, robbery, causing hurt, murder, rape, adultery, which are covered by the modern civil and criminal laws under various systems of law, fall under anyone or more of the four evil verbal actions or three wicked bodily actions as analysed by Manu. The several provisions made in the *Manusmṛti* follow this basic analysis. Before laying down the code of conduct for implicit obedience by individuals and the penalty for disobedience at the hands of the king (the State), Manu cautions everyone to have self-control, so that his mind does not act as the instigator for committing any sinful mental action which would inevitably lead to one or the other type of evil verbal actions or wicked bodily actions.'

' In the present times, human beings are subjecting others to untold misery and agony by their evil actions perpetrated for purely selfish ends. In particular onslaught and assault on women are on the increase and this is heinous and most degrading. For such purposes, they are using the most modern arms and ammunitions. Everyday newspapers carry news of such atrocities committed by individuals for one reason or the other. Thus, scientific inventions which are intended to be a boon to humanity are becoming a curse. Why is it so? The answer is not far to seek. In fact, the reason is human beings have not been educated and trained to exercise control over the mind, speech, and bodily actions and not to inflict injury on others with a purely selfish motive. In fact, this should have been the most fundamental education to be imparted to individuals right from their childhood by which alone human beings develop the capacity to control their mind, speech, and bodily actions. Everyone should be made to realise, that for the sake of satisfying one's greed or desire one were to indulge in illegal and immoral acts, he might secure a momentary physical enjoyment, but would land himself in deep trouble by losing mental peace and happiness and thus he has to suffer throughout his life.' It is by such education only that the character of an individual can be moulded so that he lives a useful, purposeful and honest life which gives him real happiness and enables him to devote his time, energy and capacities to the service of other human beings and prevents him from exploiting others for selfish ends.'

***Sāmānya Dharma*:** The meaning of the Sanskrit word *Dharma* is very wide. In fact, there is no equivalent word corresponding to *Dharma* in any of the languages of the world. All the rules of righteous conduct of human beings in every sphere of human activity evolved from times immemorial in India, fall within the meaning of the word *Dharma*, which applies to all, whether they belong to any religion or not. It is a code of conduct for all human beings for all times to come. It is eternal as indicated in *MS.* (10.63).

ahinsā satyam-asteyaṁ śaucaṁ indriyanigrahaḥ
evaṁ sāmāsikaṁ dharmaṁ chāturvarṇye abravīumanuḥ.

Ahiṁsā (non-violence), *Satya* (truthfulness), *Asteya* (not coveting the property of others), *Śaucam* (purity), and *Indriyanigraha* (control of senses) are, in brief, the common Dharma for all.

Rāja Dharma

According to Justice M. Rama Jois, 'this is equivalent to the modern Constitutional Law. *Rājadharma* regulated the power and duties of the King. It was made obligatory for the king to give equal protection to all his subjects without discrimination. On this subject,'*Manusmṛti*' (9-31) says:

यथा सर्वाणि भूतानि धरा धारयते समम्।
तथा सर्वाणि भूतानि बिभ्रतः पार्थिवं व्रतम्।।

'Just as the mother earth gives equal support to all the living beings, a king should give support to all without any discrimination.'

Again in *Bhagavadgītā*, Śri Krishna lays down the proper code of conduct by saying that a person who observes such a code of conduct is dear to Him.

'The person who hates none, who is friendly and has compassion for all, who *has* no selfishness and ego, who maintains the balance of mind in pain and pleasure, who has contentment, is steady in meditation, self-controlled, and firm in his decision, who is dedicated to me, and who is my devotee is dear to me.'

Conclusion

From the above deliberations, it candidly transpires that the *Manusmṛti* contains many gems of Vedic ethical values, which are still valid, and need due consideration for implementation in the present times, both by individuals and the Society at large. Due to the deteriorating moral standards and degradation of ethical values, modern society is probably going astray. *MS.* has many eternal ethical values of permanence, which need to be imbibed if the deteriorating trend is to be arrested. In essence, Manu dismisses any pessimism and despondency from his scheme. It is perhaps this aspect that enthused, the great philosopher, Nietzsche to exclaim about *Manusmṛti*, 'It has an affirmation of life, a triumphing agreeable sensation in life and that to draw up a lawbook such as Manu means to permit oneself to get the upper hand, to become perfection, to be ambitious of the highest art of living.'

Family Values in Manusmriti

Respect for Womanhood

Respect for women was another most cherished value of life from times immemorial in India. Women were not considered as an object of physical pleasure by man, but were regarded as *divine treasures for family life* (*MS.* 4.137). In view of the role assigned by nature to mothers, and in view of the fact that the mother is the dearest person on earth to an individual and in view of the intense love and affection of a mother for her children, and her readiness to make tremendous sacrifices for the sake of her children the mother came to be regarded as God incarnate (*Mātā Pratyakṣa Devatā).* Further, as every woman is a potential mother, the cultural value evolved was to treat the mother as God and to treat every woman except one's wife, as a mother. This value appears to have been created and cultivated assiduously as an antidote to the sexual propensity of man, for, once the value that every woman is mother is ingrained in the heart of an individual, sinful thoughts of committing any offence against woman gets destroyed. There can be no doubt that inculcating such a value in the hearts of individuals is the greatest protection against the immoral sexual desires of man. The creation and maintaining of this value is really the most valuable contribution of our ancestors.

Manusmṛti mandates in the following verses that highest respect and regard must he extended to women. Manu's numinous views on women described in the below-quoted verses are not to be found in any non-Hindu religious scripture in the annals of world civilization:

- Women must be honoured and adorned by their fathers, brothers, husbands, and brothers-in-law, who desire their own welfare (3.55).

- Where women are honoured, there the gods are pleased; but where they are not honoured, no sacred rite yields rewards (3.56).
- Where the female relations live in grief, the family soon wholly perishes; but that family where they are not unhappy ever prospers (3.57).
- The houses on which female relations, not being duly honoured, pronounce a curse, perish completely as if destroyed by magic (3.58).
- Hence men who seek (their own) welfare, should always honour women on holidays and festivals with (gifts of) ornaments, clothes, and best of food (3.59).
- In that family, where the husband is pleased with his wife and the wife with her husband, happiness will assuredly be lasting (3.60).

However, there is a verse on the basis of which *Manusmṛti* is criticized and condemned as being against women. It reads:

पिता रक्षति कौमारे भर्ता रक्षति यौवने।

रक्षन्ति स्थविरे पुत्रा न स्त्री स्वातन्त्र्यमहर्ति।। *MS.* 9.3

'The father supports the girl in her childhood, the husband supports her after marriage and her sons support her in old age. At no stage, a woman should go without support.'

Dr. Surender Kumar has disputed the genuineness of this verse being of non-Vedic origin and against the basic principles of Manu, as explained in Manu's other verses. However, according to Justice M. Rama Jois, 'On the basis of the last part of the above verse, without reference to the earlier parts and other verses in *Manusmṛti*, referred to earlier, the criticism levelled against *Manusmṛti* is that it wanted women to live like slaves of man throughout their life. Nothing can be farther from the truth. It is a matter of common knowledge that in most of the families the women are not only respected most, but their advice in every matter concerning the family also prevails and even now it is so. They shape the fortunes of the family. Therefore, the true meaning and purpose of the above verse is that a woman requires and is entitled to support in every stage of life. Correspondingly it is the duty of the father, the husband, and the sons to look after the daughter, the wife, and the mother respectively. It is the duty of the **father** to look after his daughter with all care, educate her, and celebrate her marriage. Thereafter the fundamental duty and responsibility to maintain and protect her stand shifted to her **husband**, and thereafter when he becomes aged, that duty gets shifted to the sons. In fact, protection and care is essential to male children as well as aged fathers. However, a special provision is made for women. Therefore, the real intention of the verse is to declare the obligation of the father, husband, and sons to maintain and support the daughter, the wife, and the mother respectively. It is not a directive to subjugate or dominate them. Therefore, to interpret the verse to the effect that a woman must be treated as a slave by her father during her childhood, and by her husband after her marriage and by her sons in old age, and that she should be deprived of freedom throughout her life is wholly erroneous and perverse. By nature, womanhood is tender and requires protection. She requires special care, protection, and arrangement for her education. Even with the advancement of civilization, most of the parents will be unwilling to send their daughters alone to a distant place for higher education. This is the essential difference between man and woman. Another illustration would be of great assistance. The above illustrations are not exhaustive. There are many situations in which women/girls require greater care, protection, and security. It is such a difference flowing from the nature of women, who are vulnerable to various kinds of onslaughts when left unprotected which is the basis for the above verse of *Manusmṛti.* It does not mean that women must be kept without freedom. Moreover, such an interpretation runs counter to the verses:

> 'Where women are honoured, there the gods are pleased; but where they are not honoured, no sacred rite yields rewards (*MS.* 3.56). Where the female relations live in grief, the family soon wholly perishes; but that family where they are not unhappy ever prospers (*MS.* 3.57). The houses on which female relations, not being duly honoured, pronounce a

> curse, perish completely as if destroyed by magic (*MS.* 3.58). Hence men who seek (their own) welfare, should always honour women on holidays and festivals with (gifts of) ornaments, clothes, and (dainty) food (*MS.* 3.59). In that family, where the husband is pleased with his wife and the wife with her husband, happiness will assuredly be lasting (*MS.* 3.60). 'The Ācārya is more venerable than a Upādhyāya (teacher). Father is more venerable than an Ācārya. But the mother is more venerable than the father' (*MS.* 2-145).

A combined reading of the verses quoted above indicates that women were placed at a higher position. So the real meaning is, the women should be honoured and protected. It is a humane and a duty-oriented provision, the mandate to provide security. This should not be misunderstood as making her life insecure. She should not be left open to attack by men with evil propensities, it does not mean her freedom should be jeopardised. Any meaning given to the verse to the effect that women should be denied freedom at every stage is perverse as it would be totally inconsistent with the other verses. For, if women are denied freedom and they are kept under subjugation they are bound to be in grief and tears, and as a consequence, the happiness of the family disappears. Hence, a meaning consistent with the above verses alone is appropriate.

This exposition may be completed best by quoting what **Kerry Brown** has stated in his book, "**The Essential Teachings of Hinduism**", having ascertained the real meaning of the controversial verse in Manu: 'In Hinduism, a woman is looked after not because she is inferior or incapable but, on the contrary, because she is treasured. She is the pride and power of society. Just as the crown jewels should not be left unguarded, neither should a woman be left unprotected. No extra burden of earning a living should be placed on women who already bear huge responsibilities in society; childbirth; child care, domestic well-being, and spiritual growth. She is the transmitter of culture to her children'.

The important role assigned to women has been correctly identified. It is no doubt true that times have changed, we have women who are competent in various professions, avocations, competent in business, who are competent political rulers, bureaucrats, technocrats, advocates, judges, and so on. But that is no reason to lose sight of the onerous responsibility of women of looking after the health and education of children or to forget the noble value of looking upon every woman as one's mother as that is the only powerful antidote or atrocities against women.

Following verses from Manusmṛti have also come under severe criticism :

- It is the nature of women to seduce men in this (world); for that reason, the wise are never unguarded in (the company of) females. (2.213)
- For women are able to lead astray a man; in (this) world not only a fool, but even a learned man, and (to make) him a slave of desire and anger. (MS 2.214).
- One should not sit in a lonely place with one's mother, sister, or daughter; for the senses are powerful, and master even a learned man. (2.215).

Although the above verses reaffirm the basic Indian belief of the women as a temptress, yet the cynical views expressed are purely from an ascetic's perspective. One might also view these verses disapprovingly, for aren't women too susceptible to the charms of the opposite sex? To the mind of the ascetic *Brahmacārins* (in which context these verses find mention), the veracity of the statements is unquestionable, as the vigorous ascetic (students) standard of life necessitated keeping them away from women. Hindu mythology has numerous accounts of even enlightened sages like *Vishvāmitra* falling to the temptation of beautiful *apsaras* sent over by Indra to scuttle the sage's advancements. The modern mind may cloak it in the garb of Freudian psychology. Non-conforming women on the other hand are capable of destabilizing the entire social order, especially in the Indian cultural milieu.

Manu on Marriage

Marriage in *Sanātana Dharma*, rather than means to merely gratify lust and longing, was means for both partners to walk the path of *Dharma*, in their collective quest towards *mokṣa.* It is in this respect, the Manu declares husband and wife to be verily one! (*MS.* 9.45). Religious rites are ordained in the Veda to be performed by the husband together with his wife (MS 9.96). The position of the wife as the homemaker is attributed in glowing terms by Manu: **there is no difference between the housewife and the Goddess of fortune; both illumine the home and are to be adored as such** (*MS.* 9.26). The safeguard is mentioned thus '*A maiden though marriageable should rather stay in her father's house until death, than that he should ever give her to a man destitute of good qualities*' (*MS.* 9.89). **Accept good women**, knowledge, *Dharma*, purity, noble ideas from wherever they come irrespective of social standing and position. (MS 2.244)

Dharma of Husband, wife and family life

The sanctity attached to the relationship of the husband and wife brought about by *Vivāha* (marriage) and the inseparability of their relationship was the firm foundation laid by the propounders of *Dharma*, on which the social life was constructed. This again had its source in the principle of three debts or three pious obligations. *Devaṛṇa* (pious obligation to the gods) was required to be discharged through religious sacrifices and other virtuous deeds such as making gifts to deserving people, as a householder. It was ordained that all such acts must be performed by the husband and the wife jointly. This injunction is being obeyed down to this day.

प्रजनार्थं स्त्रियः सृष्टाः संतानार्थं च मानवाः ।

तस्मात्साधारणो धर्मः श्रुतौ पत्न्या सहोदितः ।। (*MS.* 9-96)

'To be mothers were created women and to be fathers men; religious rites, therefore, are ordained in the Veda to be performed by the husband and wife together.'

MARRIAGE -A SAMSKARA

Vivaha (marriage) was one of the most important of the several 'samskaras' (sacraments) prescribed by Dharmasastras for the individual. The object and purpose of marriage as declared by Dharmasastras was not merely to satisfy the carnal desire of a man and woman though it did constitute the basis of the desire for marriage. The propounders of Dharma, after deep thought and consideration, deliberately relegated the natural carnal desire to a secondary position as they considered that greater stress on this aspect would result in the 'throw-away attitude' i.e., an attitude to give up the wife or husband, as the case may be, at the whim and fancy of either of them and go in for a new one, just as one discards an article meant for use or enjoyment after some use and goes after a new one. This they considered as injurious to the interests of the individual and society. They stressed that coming together of a man and woman was necessary for the fulfillment of the threefold ideals of life, ie., *Dharma, Artha, and Kama.* The sum and substance of these three goals was that the husband and the wife, remaining loyal to each other throughout their life, should restrain their desire (*kama*) for material pleasure, wealth, and prosperity (*Artha*) by *Dharma* (righteous rules of conduct) and should share the happiness and misery and discharge their prescribed duties towards the family and society throughout their life.

This is highlighted by a promise which a bridegroom was required to make while undergoing the vivaha Samskara. While giving the girl in marriage, the father, or in his absence the guardian, addresses the bridegroom with the following words:

धर्मे चार्थे च कामे च नातिचरितव्या त्वयेयम्।

You shall not transgress Dharma in the attainment of Artha and Kama.

The bridegroom accepts the condition with these words:

नातिचरामि

I shall not transgress Dharma, in matters of Artha and Kama.

The relationship was not merely sexual. The husband and the wife were together required to observe a code of conduct, and they had to discharge their responsibility jointly. In particular, they were together required to discharge four pious obligations namely; (i) towards God, (ii) towards parents, (iii) towards the teacher and (iv) towards humanity. This could be discharged only by living together with mutual love and fidelity throughout their life which is the sum and substance of the dharma of husband and wife. To impress upon every couple this aspect MS (9.101; 3.60) declared thus:

> अन्योन्यस्याव्यभिचारो भवेदामरणान्तिकः।
> एष धर्मः समासेन ज्ञेयः स्त्रीपुंसयोः परः।।
> संतुष्टो भार्यया भर्ता भर्त्रा भार्या तथैव च।
> यस्मिन्नैव कुले नित्यं कल्याणं तत्र वै ध्रुवम्।।

> Mutual friendship and fidelity is the highest Dharma to be observed by husband and wife, throughout their life. The family in which husband and wife have mutual affection and respect always secures happiness and prosperity.

The validity and utility of the directive for all and its eternal value are unexceptionable. The observance of the above directive throughout life by the husband and the wife is not only conducive to happiness and harmony in family life but also essential for national or social life.

Conclusion

From the above deliberations, it candidly transpires that the Manu Smriti contains many gems of Vedic ethical values, which are still valid, and need due consideration for implementation in the present times, both by individuals and the Society at large. Due to the deteriorating moral standards and degradation of ethical values, modern society is probably going astray. MS has many eternal ethical values of permanence, which need to be imbibed if the deteriorating trend is to be arrested. In essence, Manu dismisses any pessimism and despondency from his scheme. It is perhaps this aspect that enthused, the great philosopher, **NIETZSCHE** to exclaim about Manu Smriti; **It has an affirmation of life, a triumphing agreeable sensation in life and that to draw up a lawbook such as Manu means to permit oneself to get the upper hand, to become perfection, to be ambitious of the highest art of living.**

To sum up, the solution to the emerging multitude of

problems which are posing a serious threat to humanity can be found through *inter alia* following measures:

(i) *Keeping in mind the positive aspects of MS,* and disregarding the negative doubtful non-genuine interpolations which have crept in it, all of us, as individuals, should *try to imbibe the basic Vedic ethical values* enshrined in this *Dharmasastra, for our own progress, in both material and spiritual life.*

*(*ii) *Endeavour to contribute our best for the welfare of humanity,* for upliftmernt of the human society at large, by carrying out our profession, avocation, trade or business in such a way as to render service to the humanity/Society, taking only reasonable remuneration or profit, and discarding *Artha* and *Kama* not based on *Dharma (*iii) We should not cause injury to others to fulfill selfish desires, or exploiting the misery of other human beings for illegitimate gains. This should be the '*Dharma*' of every individual, and *through the improvement of the individual, we can hope to ameliorate society and humanity for a better and more happier world to live in.*

I do hope that my appeal will be given due consideration by the learned readers and through them disseminated to others concerned to pave way for the entire humanity to be happy.

REFERENCES

- Kumar, Surender, Dr.: *The Manu Smriti* (in Hindi): Arsh Sahitya Prachar Trust, Delhi(1991).
- Jois Rama, M. Justice: *Ancient Indian Law: Eternal Values in Manu Smriti*: Universal Law Publishing Co. Pvt. Ltd. (2004 Reprint)
- Jois Rama, M. Justice: *A Monograph on Dharma the Global Ethics,* website.
- Bühler, Georg*: Manu Saṁhitā: The Laws of Manu,* translated by Georg Buhler and edited by Max Mueller: The Secret Books of the East, Vol.25.

Human Values from the Bhagvadgītā

(Relevance for Modern Management)

Human and ethical values have been the very foundation of Indian scriptures, including *Bhagvad Gītā.* This paper attempts to provide some insights into the qualities (values) for *jñāna* (knowledge) espoused by Yogirāja Krisna to Arjuna, as enshrined in Chapter 13 of the *Bhagvad Gītā.* The learned author, while explaining these values, has also attempted to provide their relevance to modern management. It is hoped that these values, if sincerely put into practice, will manifest attitudinal change in the mind of the modern-day managers. Editor

The present alarming erosion of **human values** in management practices leading to ethical dilemmas could prove threatening factors for all-round development of a nation. India has the eternal wealth of human values which were taught in the *Vedas, Upaniṣads,* and *Bhagvad Gītā.* One has to inculcate and develop these human values for leading a peaceful integrated life, as also for a reorientation of various management practices for the achievement of managerial goals. Such transformation would not only better one's own life but also help to attain peace and prosperity in the practice of business in the world of corporate management. Today, the essence of human values is the nourishing factor for 'the management capability' of a manager, who is the leading figure of the management scenario.

The *Bhagvad Gītā* is the essence of the *Vedas* and *Upaniṣ ads.* One of the greatest contributions of India to the world is the *Bhagvad Gītā.* Today the ancient Indian philosophy of *Bhagvad Gītā*, which has entered *inter alia* in the managerial domain of the world, has found its place not only as an alternative to the theory of modern management but also as an inspirational source to individuals by bringing them back the right path of peace and prosperity. The management lessons from *Bhagvad Gītā* have been illumined to the world by many

Indian saints. It provides 'all that is needed to raise the consciousness of man to the highest possible level.' It reveals the deep, universal truths of life that speak to the needs and aspirations of everyone. To motivate Arjuna to do his duty, the *Bhagvad Gītā* was preached on the battlefield of *Kurukshetra* by Śri Krishna. For the present-day managers, who are facing similar ethical dilemmas, albeit, in a bit different scenario, *Bhagvad Gītā* has got all the management tools to provide the mental equilibrium and to overcome any crisis situations through inspirational messages gleaned from it. The *Bhagvad Gītā* can be experienced as a powerful catalyst for transformation. This divine book will contribute to self-reflection, finer feeling and deepen one's inner process, making the worldly life more dynamic, full of joy - no matter what the circumstances might be- through attitudinal changes in the individuals. What makes the *Bhagvad Gītā* a practical psychology of transformation is that it offers us the tools to connect with our deepest intangible essence, leading us to participate in the battle of life with the right knowledge.

In Chapter 13 of the *Bhagvad Gītā*, Śri Krishna, in response to a question by Arjuna about *jñānam* (knowledge) and *jñeyam* (that which is to be known), lists **20 qualities (values) of the mind** which must be present before the mind of the seeker. The values to be personally valuable must be discovered through knowledge (seen as valuable by the value-holder) and not simply impressed upon from without. Although the list of values constituting *jñānam* is long, yet the qualities (values) stated therein are inter-related, defining a harmonious frame of mind in which knowledge can occur. Each of them highlights a certain attitude, the value for which must be discovered personally, in order that attitude becomes a natural aspect of the seeker's frame of mind [5]. Śri Krishna declares all these to be knowledge and anything beyond these as ignorance[6].

These qualities or human values have been stated in the *Bhagvad Gītā* as follows:

amānitvam adambhitvam ahiṁsā kṣāntir ārjavam.
ācāryopāsanaṁ śaucaṁ sthairyam ātma-vinigrahaḥ. (13.7)

Humility (absence of self-worshipfulness), absence of self-glorification, non-violence (non-harmfulness), forbearance (attitude of accomodaion), straight-fordwardness, service to *Gurus*, internal and external cleanliness (cleanliness of thought, word, and deed), steadfastness, self-control; and

indriyārtheṣu vairāgyam-anahaṁkāra eva ca.
janma-mṛtyu-jarā-vyādhi-duḥkha-doṣānudarśanam. (13.8)

State of dispassion towards the objects of sense organs or the absence of compelling drive for worldly pleasures and possessions, absence of *ahaṁkāra* (ego), constant reflection on the agony and suffering inherent in birth, old age, disease, and death.

asaktir-anabhiṣvaṅgaḥ putradāra-gṛhādiṣu.
nityaṁ ca samacittatvam-aniṣt-āniṣṭopapattiṣu. (13.9)

Detachment, non-fondness with progeny, wife, and home; unfailing equanimity upon attainment of the desirable and the undesirable; and

mayi cānanyayogena bhaktiravyabhicāriṇī.
viviktadeśasevitvam aratirjanasansadi. (13.10)

Unswerving faith in (what I say) and action with complete devotion, love for solitude, distaste for social gossips; and

adhyātmajñānanityatvaṁ tattvajñānārthadarśanam.
etajjñānamiti proktam-ajñānaṁ yadato'nyathā. (13.11)

Constant absorption into spirituality (*Adhyātma*). Seeking the presence of God everywhere (who is the subject of true knowledge). This is called knowledge; what is contrary to this is known as ignorance.

jñeyaṁ yat-tatpravakṣyāmi yajjñātvāmṛtamaśnute.
anādimatparaṁ brahma na sattannāsaducyate. (13.12)

I shall say what is worth knowing, knowing which one attains immortality. The Supreme Brahman is beginning-less. He is said to be neither *Sat* nor *Asat*, (because he is indescribable) (See also 9.19).

Let us discuss these twenty values advised by Krishna to

Arjuna, to ascertain their relevance in assisting the modern management for the efficient and effective performance of various functions by the managers and guide them for ethical dilemmas faced by them.

Value 1: '*Amānitvam* (Absence of Self-Worship-fullness)

According to Swami (Dr.) Parthasarthy, *Amānitvam* originates from Sanskrit word *mānitvam,* which means extending to conceit or haughtiness. It is an exaggerated opinion about oneself. *Manaḥ* implies that whatever qualification one has looms large in one's mind as worthy of respect and regards from others. Thus, *mānitvam* stands for exaggerated self respectfulness or self worshipfulness. *Amānitvam* indicates the absence of such self-worshipfulness. A simple, factual self-respectfulness, in fact, is a good quality of mind. The problem arises only when self-respectfulness is exaggerated into self-worshipfulness, which undesirably incites others to show me the respect that I feel is my due. When I demand respect, rarely will it be given to me on my terms. The person upon whom I make such a demand may not respond. Or, he may be suffering from his own *mānitvam*, respond with hostility, or make a demand upon me for greater respect. The result can be mutual hurt, friction between each other, troubled minds.

The basis/cause of self-worshipfulness is found in a deep underlying doubt in my own mind about my own qualifications. When I am completely certain that I have, in full measure, the qualifications that I claim, I have no need to demand from others respect for them. *Mānitvam* arises because I do not seem to accept myself as one who is qualified. The demand from others for recognition shows that I need some support so that I can feel that I am somebody. This demand comes from an inner sense of emptiness, a lack of readiness to accept myself as I am because I secretly fear that what I am not good enough. I assert not just my qualifications, but my qualification in the glorified light in which I view them.

Hurt is possible when there is a 'bloated ego' or pride. An inflated ego is disproportionate, with excessive significance attached to what I know, what I feel, what I possess, what I do, how I look. With this overemphasis on a 'knower-doer-I' comes the expectation of a certain response from others recognizing my importance. When the response does not come, then comes hurt. A hurt -deflated ego tends to spend a lot of time planning how to teach a lesson to the one who brought about the hurt, and ..... with a lot of hurts, the list of those who have to be taught a lesson is likely to be long. For such a person, sitting quietly in meditation is not possible. In such a firmament of the mind, the luminaries are all the people who caused hurt; and it is upon them that he dwells in meditation. A hurt mind is like a monkey's wound, which does not heal but only gets reopened.

It is fine to have abilities and to use them; but abilities should be allowed to speak for themselves. *My attitude towards my accomplishments should be like a flowering bush towards its blossoms. It blooms because it must bloom.* And this is the way I should be about my gifts and skills. I should simply use them as best I can because that seems to be what I am supposed to do. People who have a value for these particular abilities may give me some respect for them, (while) others who have no value for these particular abilities, no doubt, will ignore them. I should let my actions themselves command respect from those who are able and willing to extend it, but I should never demand respect.

A manager, who is imbibed with the value of *amānitvam,* will be shorn of complexities, and, therefore, have lesser conflict situations, as people will respect him for his /her qualities of their own and extend cooperation towards the achievement of organizational goals. On the contrary, if he/she seeks *mānitvam* (self-worshipfulness) the concerned persons shall start doubting his credentials and not respect him spontaneously.

Value 2: *Adambhitvam* (Absence of Self-Glorification)

Adambhitvam is the mental attitude in which *damba* is absent. *Dambha* is an expression quite similar to the *mānitvam,* namely, manifestation of self-glorification, although the foundation of the expression differs, *while mānitvam's conceit is an expression based on real achievements and abilities, the claim to fame caused by dambha stems from pretended or fabricated accomplishment and abilities.* Thus, a *dambhi* is one who claims achievements that are not his or pretends to possess abilities which he does not have. It is called *dambha* when I trumpet my glory for what is not there when by design I give the impression that I am something, which I know I am not. *Dambhitvam* (*self-glorification*) brings with it the need to be ever alert and to have a long memory, while truth does not require any special remembering.

A manager inspired with the value of *adambhitvam,* will have spontaneous respect from his/her colleagues and subordinates to elicit the best of cooperation from them. In contrast, the one who has the negative value of *dambhitvam* (self-glorification) will not be able to inspire adequate confidence to be an effective manager/leader, as his very attitude based on falsehood, which pretence does not long last, will expose him/her in the eyes of the concerned person and slur his image.

Value 3: '*Ahiṁsā*' (Non-Harmfulness)

Ahiṁsā means 'non-injury or non-harmfulness,' and reflects one's desire to live free of hurt or pain or threat of any sort. If I know that someone holds hurtful thoughts about me, I feel hurt, despite such thoughts being not expressed in deeds or words. *Ahiṁsā* means not causing harm by any means: by deeds *kāyena*, by words, *vācā,* or by thought, *manasā.* The moot point that *why should I not hurt other beings is because I do not want to be hurt myself. Commonsense ethics dictates that I can not do unto others what I do not want to be done to me.* So *Ahiṁsā*, non-injury becomes a value for me. *Ahiṁsā* is simple commonsense *dharma*, confirmed by the Vedas, and by all scriptures but subject to interpretation. If an act which is literally injurious is otherwise meant for the benefit of another, such as the cut of the surgeon's knife is not *hiṁsā.* In a relative world, absolute *ahiṁsā* is not possible.

Vegetarianism is an example of the application of the value

of *ahiṁsā.* In India, where there are more vegetarians than anywhere else in the world, vegetarianism is squarely based on the *Vedic* mandate: *hiṁsāṁ na kuryāt-* do not harm others. For the man, unlike animals, whose self-consciousness brings into play a will that is free to choose many means to meet life's ends, including the basic need, food. Being not pre-programmed, man must choose the kind of food he eats. *There is also evidence that human dental and digestive systems are more suitable for a fruit, grain, vegetable diet than for meat.* They have fewer degenerative diseases and live longer, and enjoy a more vigorous old age than do their meat-eating neighbours. Moreover, all living beings have a value for life and seek to live harm-free. Animals, birds, fish- all mobile creatures- run away when they know I am trying to catch them for the stew pot. When I do catch them, they struggle and cry. Therefore, it is evident that they do not want to be hurt, that they want to live. Since I have been given free will to choose the food to sustain myself, I must find some norm to guide me in choosing that food. The gift of free will carries with it a responsibility to follow an ethical norm in the exercise of that will. *My commonsense dharmic norm for the choice of food tells me that I should not make 'somebody' my dinner since I do not want to be somebody's dinner.* Those who cry in protest or struggle against me are more 'somebody' than plants rooted in one place, which quietly give up their fruits for my food, normally without even surrendering their lives. Thus, plant food is the rational/ethical choice for the human diet.

With such finer appreciation of feelings of others by inculcating this golden values of *Ahiṁsā*, a manager becomes adequately sensitized to handle human element in the enterprise more effectively, minimizing the conflict situations adequately. Through *Ahiṁsā* by causing no harm by any means: by deeds, by words, or by thought, the manager becomes proactive enough to have more friends, both within the organization and outside, to build more and more bridges of understanding (than misunderstanding) and reap full advantage through this positive endeavour, both for himself and his organization.

Value 4: *Kṣānti* (Attitude of Accommodation)

The attitude of *kṣānti* means that I cheerfully, calmly accept the extraction or demand that another person (or situation) should make, in order to conform to what I think would be pleasing to me. I accommodate situations and people happily. *All relationships require accommodation.* The value must be built upon an understanding of the nature of people and the relationships between them. I will never find in one person all qualities which I like, or all qualities which I dislike, having a mixture of things which I find appealing and others which I find non-appealing. Similarly, I am also both appealing and non-appealing. No one is going to find me totally likeable.

When I recognize these facts, I will see that every relationship is going to require some accommodation from me. I am not going to be willing or, perhaps, be able to change and meet all expectations other people have from me, nor are they for themselves. In particular, relationships with such things which I strongly dislike, require accommodation from me. If I can change the person or can put distance between him/her and me without avoiding duty, that is fine. But if I can not, I simply must accommodate happily, taking the person as he/she is. *I can expect neither the world nor the people to change in order that I may be happy.* It is just not possible to compel people to change to meet my image of what they should be like. More often than not, when I want a change from others, they will just as strongly want a change from me. It will be a standoff. Hence, the need for an attitude of *kṣānti* or accommodation.

Kṣānti (accommodation) is a beautiful and saintly quality. *Among all the qualities, ahiṁsā and kṣānti constitute the qualities of a saint.* One need not have wisdom, one need not have scriptural learning to be a saint, but one must have these two values. A saint is a person who never consciously hurts another person by action, word or thought, and who accepts people - good or bad - just as they are. He is the one who has an endless capacity to be accommodative, forgiving, merciful, which are included in the quality (or value) called *kṣānti,* which attitude expands one's heart. Through *kṣānti,* the heart becomes so commodious, it accommodates all people and circumstances just as they are, without desire or demand that they be different[10].

As a manager, in order to discover within myself a value for accommodation, I should look at the person behind the act, and respond to the person, not to the action. Usually, when I am responding to the behaviour of the person, or to his action, I find it difficult to be accommodative. But when I try to understand the cause behind the action (e.g. what is behind the fit of anger or outburst of jealousy or domineering manner) and respond to the person (not to his actions), I find it easy to be accommodative, and the potential conflict situations are minimized.

Value 5: *Ārjvam* (Straight-forwardness)

Ārjavam means 'straightness.' When used as a value, 'straightness' or *ārjavam* is like the English word rectitude (from the Latin word *rectus*, straight), which means 'conduct in accordance with one's thought and words.' *When there is rjubhāva (arrow-like straightness) between a physical action and the word, or between the word and the thought, the alignment is called ārjavam.* When I think of one thing and say another, or when I say one thing and do another, or when I think about one thing and do yet another third thing, all of these constitute a non-alignment of thought, words, and deeds on my part. Avoidance of this gap, this division between word and action, word and thought, and action and thought, is *ārjavam*. *Ārjavam* can be considered to be an extension of *satya vacanam*, truthful speech. *Ārjavam* includes not just speech but thoughts and actions also. For *ārjavam,* my actions must be true to my words and my words true to my thoughts.

A manager shorn of this value with a splintered and disintegrated personality can not perform the leadership role, as nobody will trust and respect him and a crisis of confidence may emerge, where both his seniors and juniors may find him a suspect and unreliable. In contrast, if he sincerely imbibes the *ārjavam* value, he will certainly be a honourable person to be reliable and worthy enough to become a leader of his team.

Value 6: *Ācāryopāsanam* (Service to the Teacher)

Ācaryopāsanam, which primarily means 'service to the teacher', is a value that is deeply embedded in Indian culture. Its intensity and universality within the culture show the high regard for knowledge and for the teacher who imparts it. It is also used to indicate specific aspects of the student-teacher relationship, including *Gurukula vāsa.* 'Meditation upon the teacher', which means meditation upon the teachings by keeping the teacher(*ācārya*), who stands for the vision of the teaching in one's heart. 'Service and surrender' is, however, the general meaning of *ācāryopāsanam,* in which sense Śri Krishna uses the term when talking to Arjuna. However, it requires a certain discrimination in its exercise and care must be taken in choosing, as it can lead to exploitation of the value holder, if the teacher is not a responsible person.

In the management scenario, both the manager and his subordinates need to inculcate this value by respecting their seniors from whom they have learnt many professional aspects of management. Such a spirit of service paves the way not only to teach and learn more but also better understanding and communication among them. Service to the teacher (*ācāryopāsanam)* is a beautiful value as it inculcates a spirit of gratitude towards the teacher/person from whom the particular knowledge or skill has been acquired.

Value 7: '*Śaucam*' (Internal and external cleanliness)

Śaucam is cleanliness in a two-fold sense: *bāhya,* outer cleanliness, and *antara,* inner cleanliness. The former is a well-understood universal value. It is easy to see the benefit that comes to me and to others from external cleanliness. Clean body, clean clothes, and a clean dwelling place makes the life more pleasant. In addition, the daily discipline of maintaining cleanliness brings about a certain attentiveness and alertness of mind.

Antara saucam, internal cleanliness, which means cleanliness of *antaḥkaraṇa,* is less easily recognized. What makes the mind *aśaucam* or unclean? Jealousy, anger, hatred, fear, selfishness, self-condemnation, guilt, pride, possessiveness, all these negative reactions and the climate of despair and resentment which comes in their wake, are the unseemliness, the *śaucam*, of the mind. Like my body gets daily *aśaucam* in my transactions with people and circumstances, similarly linked to my *ragas* and *dveṣas* (likes and dislikes, which produce desires and aversions), smudges of envy settle, a spot of exasperation lands, streaks of possessiveness appear, and overall, the fine dust of self-criticism, guilt and self-condemnation spreads into my mind. Like I maintain daily external cleanliness, each day, my mind must be cleaned until my false identification with the mind goes, in the knowledge of the Self. When there is no daily cleaning outside or inside, the accumulation makes the task much more difficult.

We can clean the mind through *pratipakṣa bhāvanā*, which means by being proactive and deliberately taking the 'opposite point of view' and willingly think the opposite of the unclean thought. Suppose, someone may do an improper action that insults or injures me. A resentment settles in my mind, which is my *aśaucam* of the mind. Allowed to remain, this resentment can build up to hatred, a painful, disturbing mental state. Seeing, therefore, the personal consequences of allowing *aśaucam* to remain, when the object of resentment comes to my attention, I summon the will to think thoughts opposite to the negative thoughts that first came to my mind. By analysis, I see that the person I resent is not disliked by anyone. Deliberately I search for reasons why others like him. I think of positive facts and call to mind whatever good things I know of him. Therefore, to clean the mind of resentment and dislikes which solidify into hatred, it is essential for a deliberate search for those things in another person which indicate his humaneness, his saintliness, they are there in everyone. Saintly qualities are the qualities of the Self, the qualities which really constitute human nature. Negative qualities are incidental; they come and go. Seeing the person behind the action from such *pratipakṣa bhāvnā* (opposite viewpoint) will discover an attitude of *kṣānti*, accommodation towards him as well. *Pratipakṣa bhāvanā* is a daily act for the mind. A mind kept clean in this manner will be a quiet and alert mind. A clean, quiet, alert mind is comfortable with itself and ready to learn, to be taught.

In the case of **Selfishness**, the *pratipakṣa bhāvanā* thoughts can often be reinforced by action as well. When I see in myself non-consideration for the wants, needs, happiness of others, I can deliberately program myself to overdo in the opposite direction, by making myself alert to the needs and happiness of those around me.

A manager, who imbibes the value of *aśaucam,* including internal cleanliness, will be more proactive and adequately sensitized to appreciate the others point of view, and therefore, shorn of selfishness, jealousy, self-condemnation, and be more effective in dealing with conflict situations and ethical dilemmas.

Value 8: *Sthairyam* (Steadfastness):

Sthairyam is *niṣṭhā,* 'firmness' or 'steadiness'. Derived from the Sanskrit root 'stha' 'to stand', *sthairyam* indicates constancy or perseverance. *Sthairyam* is: *Karma niṣṭhā, swadharma niṣṭhā* i.e. 'steadfastness in action, steadfastness in one's duty.' Thus, a steady effort on one's part toward committed goals or toward duties or responsibilities imposed upon one, is *sthairyam.* When it comes to applying effort towards a goal, most of us find ourselves to be *arathbhasuraḥ,* that is, 'heroes at the beginning'. We start any undertaking very bravely; we are lions of resolution at first, but then enthusiasm wanes. The energy of the 'heroic beginner' dwindles when the total effort required becomes clear. Then, some pretext is found to escape the completion of the job. Lack of steadiness towards a commitment results in goals not being achieved. This brings a build-up of guilt over failure to complete what was started. *Sthairyam* means there should be a steady effort towards whatever you have committed ourselves to achieve until it is achieved. Thus, it is a steadiness that neither yields to laziness nor is disturbed by distraction.[14]

In the management context, *sthairyam* highlighted is *niṣṭhā* or firmness not only in seeking the total content of all knowledge, in which all other goals resolve but also total commitment and steadfastness in one's duty through appropriate and timely action, in which *sthairyam*; steadiness is a prerequisite. Without this golden value, the manager simply can not survive. He need imbibe the value of *sthairyam* constancy or perseverance and be steadfast in both planning and action.

Value 9: *Ātmavinigrha* (Mastery over the Mind)

Ātmavinigraha, means mastery over the mind. The Sanskrit word *'ātma'* signifies the first person singular 'I'. It can be used for the physical body or its vital functions; the mind or its 'ego' sense can also be called *ātmā.* Here, in the context of Śri Krisna's instructions to Arjuna, *ātmā* simply means the mind of the *antaḥkarṇa. Vinigraha* means 'restraint' or 'curbing', which, with reference to this value is 'mastery' of the mind. *What must be mastered is one's way of thinking.* The mind is a colourful kaleidoscope of fanciful thoughts which come and go, as the mind is whimsical by nature. But I, the thinker, need not fulfill the fancies or yield to the caprices, as I am the sanctioning authority.

In general, thinking of mind is of three types: **Impulsive**, in which unexamined thoughts born of instinct hold sway; **mechanical,** in which prior conditioning is the dictator; and, **deliberative**, wherein my buddhi, the evaluating function of mind, consciously examines my thoughts, accepting or dismissing them in accordance with my value structure. There is a fourth way of thinking - **spontaneous,** in which my thoughts without deliberation, conform to the highest universal values. Spontaneous thinking of this kind manifests at an absolute level only in one who has Self-knowledge. *At a relative level, spontaneous thinking reflects the degree to which universal values have become my personal and assimilated values.* In essence, spontaneous thinking is complete *ātmavinigraha.* It is only knowledge of the Self that can completely destroy the hold of the likes and dislikes that compel and condition the way of thinking. *Complete mastery is characterized by spontaneity.*

Sāma, dāma, and *samādhāna* are Sanskrit terms often used to indicate different aspects of *ātmavinigraha. Sāma* is understood to mean discipline overthinking at the level where the thoughts arise, *dāma* indicates choice exercised over thoughts and actions at the level of sense organ expression. *Samādhāna* means *cittaikāgratā*, which literally indicates single pointed-ness of the mind. *Cittaikāgratā* is the art of applying the mind consistently to a given pursuit for a length of time. The art of *Samādhāna* or *cittaikāgratā* can then be learned by beginning to apply the mind with a sharpened awareness of distractions. The whole of *ātmavinigraha* is a matter of alertness and awareness. If I am alert and conscious of what my mind is doing, I always have a choice over my way of thinking. *With choice, I can change and can conform my behaviour to values, learn from mistakes, and can hold to commitments in the face of distraction.*[15]

A manager should necessarily have the complete mastery of his/her mind by imbibing this golden value of *ātmavinigraha*. Being endowed with spontaneous thinking (where universal values become personal and assimilated values) he/she is shorn of personal likes and dislikes to have a dispassionate view of all the emerging situations and deal with the problems effectively. If his judgment is clouded with personal prejudices without *ātmavinigraha*, his decisions may become arbitrary, affecting the overall functioning of the organization adversely. *Ātmavinigraha* may be candidly relevant to the manager at the corporate level while facing ethical dilemmas.

Value 10: *'Indriyārtheṣu Vairāgyam'* (State of Dispassion towards the Object of Sense Organs)

As explained by Dr. Parthasarthy *Indriyārtheṣu Vairāgyam* means a 'state of dispassion towards the objects of sense organs' or the absence of compelling drive for worldly pleasures and possessions'. *Rāga* is more than just a fancy or preference; it is a craving for something. One who is free from such cravings is called vairāgī and his bhāva - the state of mind - is called *vairāgyam*. Dispassion is, however, not a state of inner suppression. It is (rather) a serene state of mind characterized by total objectivity towards the things of the world, the objects of the senses. Dispassion is gained by clearly seeing objects for just what they are: by seeing, without subjective distortion, just how objects relate to me, to my happiness and welfare.

Basically, a human being seems to find himself to be a wanting person, with all compelling desires turn upon this human sense of want. That I want to be a complete person and which, I am not (as I am), is the common human experience. *Seeing myself as incomplete, unfulfilled, inadequate, insecure, I try to bring completeness to myself by the pursuit of pleasures and acquisition of things.* I devote myself to two of the fundamental human pursuits - the struggle for *kāma* and that for *artha*. *Kāma* in Sanskrit stands for all sorts of desires. *Kāma* indicates not just eating, but gourmet eating; not just drinking, but drinking as a compelling pleasure. *Artha* stands for all means to satisfy desires.

In the management context, a manager with a serene state of mind characterized by total objectivity towards the things of the world, including the objects of the senses, can have a dispassionate view through non-attachment with *artha* and *kāma,* to steer clear of all the ethical dilemmas faced by him. If he/she gets swayed by the worldly objects of the senses, disregarding *indriyarthesu vairāgyam,* there is no end to his ethical dilemmas, as recently faced by Mr. Paul Wolfowitz, who has to resign as the World Bank President, having favoured his companion lady employee for her high paying promotion. Such examples at the corporate level, both within India and abroad, abound to show how passions of the senses have brought bad name both to the individuals and the institutions concerned.

Value 11: *Anahaṅkāra* (Absence of Self-egotism)

Anahaṅkāra means 'absence of the sense of *ahaṅkāra,* freedom from an individualized I-identification. It indicates the conception of one's own individuality (i.e. 'I do', 'I own, 'I enjoy'). Total destruction of *ahaṅkāra* means Self-knowledge. However, *Anahaṅkāra* has been included here as one of the values which prepares the mind for gaining knowledge, and has a relative meaning as a means preparatory for knowledge. *Ahaṅkāra* is ego, whose presence is the sheer result of ignorance. The ego gains its status because I never think of examining its reality. When I clearly, objectively examine the claims made by ego, it cannot but quietly deflated. Ignorance is not something to which I proudly lay claim. My claim to knowledge is (also) spurious. Knowledge is not anything created by me, but only discovered in the wake of the loss of ignorance. Knowledge is always there. No one owns or creates knowledge. To be knowledgeable is only a matter of shedding ignorance. I can never be the author of knowledge. In fact, no one can be the author of knowledge. That is why Vedas (knowledge) are called *apauruṣeyas* (not created/authored by human beings). Nor can I assign to *Ahaṅkāra* personal credit for skill or speed in shedding ignorance. Certain preset factors condition my learning opportunities. Parents, teachers, neighbours, schools, various experiences, all contribute to the removal of my ignorance. *Ahaṅkāra*, the ego does not create the people or circumstances but claims the result.

Ahaṅkāra (ego), and *manitvam* (pride), are closely related, both born out of the same cause, that is ignorance of the relationship of the individualized sense of 'I' with the world. The result of any act of mine occurs both as the product of materials which I have not authored. Pride and ego, when analytically examined, become so silly that humility really cannot be considered a virtue. When I understand things as they are, I will be neither proud nor will I will be self-condemning. Self-condemnation also is an expression of *ahaṅkāra* (ego), as it is *antara aśaucam*, an impurity of the mind, to be cleaned by understanding that there is no locus for condemnation other than a particular thought. In the correct understanding of myself and my relationship to the world, there is no room for either pride or self-condemnation. The world is filled with wonderful opportunities. Therefore, I make use of this vehicle of body-mind, etc., as a source of learning to the best of my ability. It is my means of shedding ignorance. I see that personal credit for anything is irrelevant and cannot be substantiated. I simply enjoy the world as a field of the discovery of knowledge, without pride, without egotism. This is the attitude of *Anahaṅkāra*.[17]

A manager endowed with such an attitude of *Anahaṅkāra* will have quite a proactive and objective mind to take various managerial decisions, and, therefore, the least conflict situations to confront and smooth sailing in having his/her various management functions performed effectively.

Value 12: *Janma-mṛtyu jarā-vyādhi duḥkha doṣa-nudarśanam* (Repeated Review of Process of Life-Death-Old Aging-Ailments-Pain)

According to Swami (Dr.) Parthasarthy, this Sanskrit word, *janma-mṛtyu jarā-vyādhi-duḥkha-doṣa-anudarśanam,* stands for a certain rigorously (pursued) objective attitude towards life. *Anudarśanam* means 'seeing again-and-again' of the *doṣa,* the 'faults' or 'defects', in life itself, from birth to death. Life begins with *janma,* along with comes *mṛtyu,* death, the inseparable mirror-twin of birth. In between are other *doṣas* viz. *jarā,* old age. The longer you elude *mṛtyu,* the more certainly a time will come when your hearing will grow dull, vision grows dim, steps unsteady, you may be comfortable while sitting, but uncomfortable while lying down, you may have an eating problem, digestion problem, thinking problem. It is old age, which always jars, and it is always round the corner.

There are two other *doṣas, vyādhi and duḥkha,* which may introduce themselves to you in infancy, perhaps even before birth. *Vyādhi* means disease; *duḥkha* means pain. *Vyādhi,* disease, is something that goes with you all the time, being not limited to a particular time or age. Similarly, *duḥkha,* pain, which is a life-long companion, means all forms of pain - physical or mental, small or large, including the grief over the loss of a loved one. Pain, like disease, cannot be avoided. Pain or trouble coming from inside are *ādhyātmika,* and from the outside *ādhibhautika,* and from an astronomical source *ādhidavika. Ādhyātmika duḥkha* (internal pain) comprises the aches and pains and troubles of my individualized person, while *adhibhautika duḥkha* (external pain) is made up of the problems of the world around me, and *ādhibhautika duḥkha* is the painful result of an event over which there is no control whatsoever, like a tidal wave or an erupting volcano. Therefore, we should bear in mind the nature of life, which is uncertain, painful, and swiftly moving towards old age and death. Keep your mind on your purpose of life. Don't fritter it away. Remember time, *kāla,* is the devourer of the world: *kāla jagadbhakṣakaḥ.*

Thus, this value exhorted by Śri Krisna to Arjuna*: janma-mṛtyu jarā-vyādhi-duḥkha-doṣa-anudarśanam,* is an important value. It is not negative but simply factual. Its purpose is to direct your attention to the need to see life objectively just as it is so that you will be able to make (the best) use of the precious time available in your hands right now. Make use of time consciously and you won't find one day, that time has passed over you and suddenly you are old. By making use of time alertly, consciously, you are a *Swami* of time, a master of time.[18]

No manager worth his salt can probably ignore such a value, while discharging his managerial responsibilities. Unless he makes the best use of the precious time available right now consciously in a planned manner, he can not succeed in achieving the organizational goals effectively.

Value 13: *Anāsakti* (Non-attachment)

Anāskti means the absence of an attitude of ownership, particularly that anything belongs to me. While ownership is notional, possession is factual. *Anāsakti* is reduction of all the relationships involving claims of ownership to factual relationships. The analysis shows that no claim to ownership can survive close scrutiny. Nothing is really mine. I cannot claim exclusive permanent title to anything - to land, to knowledge, to people, to things, or even to my own body-mind unit. For example, my house, which is made up of the materials available in an existent creation, assembled by or in accordance with the knowledge of countless human beings, is simply an aggregate structure available for my temporary possession and control. Similarly, even for my own body, to which my mother, father, society, my wife, son, etc. may claim creation or ownership, I am just an in-dweller of this body and its managing trustee. Even the laws of the state recognize that bodies are entrusted and prohibit suicide, reflecting the recognition that the person has no right to kill, and has the right to maintain it but not to destroy it, a possessive right only to make use of it. Thus, a possessor's attitude, (whether it be towards house, money, or one's own body), rather than an ownership attitude, towards anything is a relief. A possessor's attitude with a factual perspective promotes dispassion and objectivity. This is the right attitude towards my mind, towards any wealth, towards the people around me. To all of them, I relate myself with *Anāsakti*, with no clinging attachment or attitude of ownership. *Anāsakti,* non-attachment, by seeing one's relationship to things objectively, is another example of *vairāgya*, dispassion. In *Anāsakti,* the dispassion highlighted is towards the relationship between oneself and the things, by discovering that there can be no valid nor lasting attachment (or ownership) to anything.[19]

This value of *Anāsakti,* non-attachment, if practiced consciously by the manager will help him/her in imbibing a more balanced attitude towards ethical dilemmas. Coupled with the concepts of performance of duties with *Niṣkāma bhāva* and the value of *Anahaṅkāra,* this can prove a golden value for the modern-day manager, who is presently more obsessed with results in the competitive business environment and likely to develop an attachment with the associated endeavours.

Value 14: *Anabhiṣvaṅga putra-dārā-gṛhādiṣu* (Non-excessive attachment towards son, wife and house)

Abhiṣvaṅga is the kind of intense attachment or affection one feels for what is particularly beloved such as *putra,* a son, *dārā,* one's wife, or *gṛha* one's house, and all other people and things usually very dear. *Abhiṣvaṅga* is, therefore, *atisneha.* So, here, *anabhiṣvaṅga* means the absence of an obsessive, sticky attachment for those certain people or things generally considered very dear. Essentially, *anabhiṣvaṅga*, as a value, means 'dispassionate caring'. With the understanding born of *Anāsakti,* freedom from ownership, one will have *anabhiṣ vaṅga,* lack of excessive attachment towards family, but no lack of dispassionate care and affection[20]

A manager should inculcate the value of *anabhiṣvaṅga,* avoiding excessive attachment towards the near and dear ones, with due dispassionate care and affection for them, during the discharge of his/her duties and responsibilities towards the organization. Moreover, when confronted with ethical dilemmas in making decisions, the interests of dear ones need to be judged dispassionately and ignored, if necessary, if these clash with the overall organizational interests.

Value 15: *Nityaṁ Samacittatvam Iśat-anistopapattiṣu* (Steadfastness of Mind)

Samacittatvaṁ Iśat-anistopapattiṣu simply means that one greets with 'sameness of mind' the results one likes or dislikes. *Sama* means 'equal', *Cittatva* means 'state of mind'. *Iśat-anistopapattiṣu* indicates the happening of something considered desirable or undesirable. So, here Śri Krisna tells Arjuna: to always maintain sameness of mind in the face of the desirable or the undesirable. Neither get elated over getting what you want nor feel dejected when you get what you do not want. Accept results as they come, factually. If some venture fails, look at the facts, learn from them if you can, and do whatever is now needed. View all situations as they occur, factually, with a mind unshaken by emotional intensity- a mind that simply decides what is to be done and directs the doing of it. When something happens that you like, don't get elated. A mind that reaches ecstasy over getting what it thinks, its wants will also hit the bottom when loss or failure occurs.

Samacittatvam is the state of mind which does not swing between elation and depression but remains in equilibrium regardless of the situation. When I face every situation with such a mind, I will meet the situation objectively. The attitude of *Samacittatvam* is another example of reducing subjective response to factual acceptance. More often than not, we resist accepting facts. When we refuse to accept facts, facts become problems. The factual response is the approach to situations of a truly practical person. As a manager, my job is to greet all the facts with a sameness of mind. This is real human strength, which is not found in powerful miracles but in the quiet mind of the one who faces the situations as they are. As I reduce situations to facts without projection of my emotional reactions upon them, my mind assumes a poise that makes it easier to appreciate the vision of *Vedānta*, which teaching distinguishes the apparently real and unfolds the nature of Reality itself. Such a mind, without subjective reaction, simply, quietly determines what needs to be done in a particular situation.[21]

We can very well visualize how successful and effective such a manager will be, who is imbibed with the golden value of *Nityam Samacittatvam Iśat-anistopapattiṣu.* With the steadfastness of mind inculcated through such value his/her decisions will be par excellence. In contrast, one with a wavering mind and lacking steadfastness is destined to prove failure.

Value 16: *Mayi ca Ananyayogena Bhaktiḥ Avyabhicāriṇī* (Steady Devotion Towards good advice)

This expresses the value of steadfast devotion to the good advice, a devotion characterised by non-separateness from the good. The non-separateness from the good can be seen in two ways: first, *ananyayoga*, the good advises cannot be separated from me, which view comes when I know the truth of goodness. Goodness is never away from me. Goodness is always around me; It is in me. It is indeed me. For me, there is no refuge other than goodness.

Such devotion is very helpful in preparing the mind for Self-knowledge. When I view all results as coming to me directly from the goodness, *samacittavaḥ*, the sameness of mind will come. Whatever happens, I will see it as *prasāda*, a blessing of goodness. This graceful acceptance of whatever comes out of goodness is called *prasāda-buddhi.* There is no regret; there is no failure; there is no elation; there is no depression. The attitude is simply grateful, graceful acceptance. This kind of devotion frees one from any kind of reaction. Experience is a good teacher for the person with a mind clear of reactions, a mind attentive and available to be taught.[21]

In the management scenario, one may view with positive benefits accruing from the attitude of 'graceful acceptance of whatever comes from goodness, with no regret, no elation, no depression on failure, leaves the mind clear of reaction, making it more proactive, attentive and receptive to be taught', makes this value worth trying. In fact, such an attitude will provide to a manager with a dispassionate and objective frame of mind to view things in the right perspective, without being attached to the outcome of his/her deliberations.

Value 17: *Vivikta Deśa Sevitvam* (Love for Spending Time in Solitary)

Vivikta deśa sevitvam is 'love for a quiet place.' It is a value for resorting to a secluded place. It is not the separateness of the place that makes the value. The value thing is the kind of mind which is happy with such a place. A mind which appreciates quiet and solitude is a mind that has a love for being with itself. This is a beautiful attitude which is not found very often in our society. We (usually) try to escape because we are not satisfied with ourselves. Therefore, we keep the mind busy so that there is no time place, or quiet in which we can be with ourselves. For some, the avenue for escape may be wanderlust, while for others drugs, gambling, or drinking. Whether harmful or seemingly benign, the need to escape betrays a reluctance on one's part to face oneself. However, a person who enjoys being with himself in quietude is not a sad person. He is a simple quiet, contemplative person. To be contemplative means to be able to face yourself happily. For the one who wants Self-knowledge, it is very important to have a value for being with oneself, for quietude. So, I learn to be with myself by willingly taking myself to a quiet place where take stock of myself and learn to love and accept myself. By inculcating the habit of repairing to a quiet place, you are learning to be with yourself, come to terms with yourself. Clear knowledge of yourself is then possible.[22]

Imagine a situation in which a manager is totally devoid of solitude and is constantly working in a noisy and distracting environment, in which he is not able to concentrate at all. He will not be able to contemplate on a serious emerging situation, and, therefore, deprived of making the correct decision, is not left quite free to be with himself. The value of *vivikta deśa sevitvam* is 'love for a quiet place' is obvious in such situations to the managers. Thus Gītā recommends meditation rooms for managers or *sādhakas*. Hope this will be the future scenario.

Value 18: *Aratiḥ janasaṁsadi* (Non-Inclination Towards People and Company)

Rati means 'love for something' or 'inclination towards' it. *Arati* indicates a lack of inclination towards something. *Jana* stands for people (male or female), and *saṁsadi* means in 'assembly'. So, this value means a lack of craving for the company, not reveling in company, not courting company, distancing from the crowd. It is not a value that calls for hatred of company or that one should dislike being around people. If the people are there, fine, be happy in their presence. But know that you do not require people to be happy. *Vivikta deśa sevitvam* (love of quietude, in which one is happy with oneself), and *aratiī janasaṁsadi* (non- reveling in the presence of company), are companion values, complementing each other. It is not that a quiet place in itself is intrinsically something good, or that the presence of company is something bad. But the values are for a happy, non-securing mind that loves being with itself. It neither revels nor hates company. With these values, I will have composure whether I am with people or without them. Someone who seeks seclusion out of hatred of people is not expressing these values. But on the other extreme, courting the company of people all the time, trying to escape from oneself, is not any more desirable than the fear of people. So, an attitude that is desired is not hatred of people but a simple love of quietude. That is, because I love to be with myself I do not court company.

This attitude establishes the right frame for a contemplative mind- for a mind given to *vicāra*, the inquiry into the basic profound questions about myself. Who am I? What is this creation? Who is God? What is the relationship between me, God, and the creation? Such an inquiry requires special sensitivity of the mind. To appreciate the knowledge of the Self, to see the Self for the non- objectifiable wholeness which requires a mind that is contemplative and sensitive. The mind should be highly sensitive, but not the sensitivity characterised by getting hurt at every turn. Values come when I thoroughly understand my relationship with people, places, and things around me. Pride and pretence, which court hurt, drop away from me; and non-harmfulness and accommodation, which soften hurt, become natural to me. *Vivikta deśa sevitvam,* resorting to a quiet place, and *aratiḥ janasaṁsadi* absence for the need for a company, are attitudes which establish such a contemplative mind centered on Self-knowledge.[23]

On the superficial level, a manager imbibing such values (Like *aratiḥ janasaṁsadi* lack of craving for company and *Vivikta deśa sevitvam* (love of quietude) may be considered a failure in dealing with people (both inside and outside the organization). However, if we think of the imperative need of his/her being contemplative in certain situations, where he requires to be left with himself, the advantage of having such golden values are obvious. Moreover, 'craving for company' itself may be unbecoming of a manager and sullen his image.

Value 19: *Tattvajñānārthadarśanam* (Keeping in View the Purpose of Knowledge of Truth)

Tattva means 'Truth' (as the irreducible reality of anything and everything), *Jñānam is* 'knowledge' (the sought-for-knowledge), *Artha* means purpose (or goal), and *Darśanam* is 'sight' or 'vision'. Thus, *tattvajñānārthadarśanam* is 'keeping in view the purpose of the knowledge of Truth'. *Tattvajñānam* (knowledge of Truth) is the *Jñeyam* of the 'things to be known' in life for which the values called *jñānārtha* prepares the mind The basic knowledge of truth can also be called the knowledge of the Self, *ātmajñānam.* In fact, this value can be described as not losing sight of Self-knowledge as one's primary goal. It also means having an overwhelming value for that goal so that it does not become eclipsed by other goals. **Self-Knowledge**, for what purpose? All human purposefulness, with collective *Sanskrit* name *puruṣārtha* (fron *puruṣa*, 'human being, and *artha,* 'purpose'), which can be classified under the fourfold human aims in life :

Dharma (Ethical standards): the goal of conforming one's behaviour to scripturally sanctioned ethical norms in order to obtain merit or avoid demerit in this life or the next; or for the one who is not adherent to any particular scriptural sanctions, simply the universal set of ethical standards maintained by human free will and shaped by one's wish to be treated in a certain manner by one's fellow human beings.

Artha (security or means): the goal of acquiring all the things which one thinks will make one secure - money, property, possessions, power, influence, name, and fame.

Kāma (pleasures/desires): the goal of enjoying the varieties of pleasures life affords - physical comforts, sensory delights, mind-pleasing escapes.

Mokṣa (liberation): the goal of discovering freedom from the hands of time - freedom from change, age, death, grief, loss; escape from a never-ending sense of inadequacy and incompleteness, from all forms of limitations; the desire to be rid of desire itself.

Looked at from the standpoint of the fourfold human aims (*puruṣārtha*), Self-knowledge *ātmajñānam* or knowledge of truth (*tattvajñānam*) does not fit into any of the first three categories. Self-knowledge is not meant for obtaining merit (puṇya) nor for the avoidance of demerit (pāpa). It is also not a commonsense ethical standard serving the interest of free-willed, self-conscious beings interacting with one another. Thus, the purpose of Self-knowledge is not to serve scriptural or commonsense ethics. Similarly, Self-knowledge does not result in the gain of either securities(*artha*) of pleasures(*kāma),* as actions, efforts are required to gain securities or pleasures. Particular knowledge shapes the effort, which does the job.

Thus, there is only one category *mokṣa* (liberation) where

tattvajñānārthadarśanam fits. Self-knowledge serves the purpose of *mokṣa.* The value of *tattvajñānārthadarśanam* means keeping in sight the goal of *mokṣa*, complete freedom from the human sense of bondage (limitation, incompleteness, inadequacy) by the seeker called *mumukṣu*, who never loses sight of the freedom he seeks or compromises or settle for a lesser thing. Swami (Dr.) Parthasarthy has very beautifully exemplified: '*like a salmon swimming out of the ocean back into the river from which it came. Where, against all odds, the fish battles the current in its single-pointed drive, back to its place of origin, so too, does the mumukṣu seek freedom- a freedom that is discovered in the knowledge of the tattva, the Truth of the origin'.*[24]

Just as a *Mumukṣu* craves for the knowledge of truth for his liberation (achievement of final goal). Similarly, a manager should be properly informed about the organisational structure so that he may take proper decisions in the interest of achieving organisational goals.

Value 20: Adhyātmajñāna Nityatvam (Stability in spirituality)

Adhyātmajñāna nityatvam, the nineteenth value in the order told by Śri Krisna to Arjuna, is discussed here as the final 20th value for the sake of more logical analysis. How does one gain the *tattvajñānārtha-darśanam,* of not losing sight of the knowledge of truth *(tattvajñānam)*, as one's primary goal? For any knowledge to be discovered there must be a valid, effective and appropriate means available to know that which is sought to be known. *Adhyātmajñana nityatvam* alone is the value, which fulfills the desire for liberation, which has matured into inquiry into *tattva,* the truth. *Adhyātma* means 'spiritual', *Jñāna* is 'knowledge'. Thus, *Adhyātmajñānam* is spirituality. *Nityatvam* is 'constancy in spirituality'. Such spirituality can be found in the teachings of Vedas, *Upaniṣads* or *Vedānta.* In fact, the very word *Upaniṣad* etymologically means *Adhyātmajñānam* (spirituality). So, the value called *Adhyātmajñāna nityatvam* (stability in spirituality or Self) is a value of constancy in spirituality.

For the present-day manager, the value like *Adhyatmajnana nityatvam,* may be required in the form of spiritual quotient. For a good manager not only an IQ (Intelligence quotient) and EQ (Emotional quotient) is required but SQ (Spiritual Quotient) will also be an additional qualification. Constancy in spirituality will help inculcate moral and spiritual values in a manager which will help him to be more of a human being instead of a machine.

Conclusion

Thus, the attitudes and ways of thinking called *jñānam* values, as specified above, have relevance for everyone, including the present-day manager. Reflecting upon them will certainly provide a keen insight and a profound grasp of the working of the mind, to make it more contemplative and steady. These basic values, if sincerely developed, shall usher a mind, which is beautiful, proactive as an objective instrument, quiet alert, and effective. It is a mind ready for any study or pursuit. Such a mind unsplit by internal conflict, undismayed by external adversity, has the best possible preparation for daily life as well as for facing the ethical dilemmas faced by the manager. Such values enhance the quality of life, whatever one's activities may be. Daily life gains efficiency and cheerfulness-even radiance- when these values are personally assimilated norms, one becomes a cheerful person, both saintly and effective. True saintliness makes one the most effective person possible in any situation or transaction, as he/she is totally objective. His /her appreciation of given circumstances is not clouded by subjective conditioning. Like a saint, such a manager *sādhaka* clearly sees the facts for what they are and can make and act upon a fact-based judgment free from the subjective interpretation or need. We may conclude this humble attempt with:

vihāya kāmān yaḥ sarvān pumāns carati niḥspṛha
nirmamo nirahaṅkāraḥ sa śāntim adhigacchati (*BG.* 2.71)

'A person who has given up all desires for sense gratification, who lives free from desires, who has given up all sense of proprietorship and is devoid of false ego - he alone can attain real peace.'[17]

References and Notes

1. Rokeach, M.: *The Nature of Human Values* : Free Press, New York (1973), p.5
2. Kar, Bijayananda, Prof.: *Value Perspective in Indian Philosophy*: Mittal Publications, New Delhi (2000); Preface page vi.
3. Gupta, N. L. Dr.: *Human Values for the 21st Century*: Anmol Pubs.Pvt. Ltd., New Delhi (2002), page 2.
4. *ibid.* page 2
5. Parthasarthy, Swami (Dr.): *Human Values and Management: 20 Key Principles for Modern Management*: Ane Books, New Delhi (2006) pp. 17-19.
6. Prabhupada Bhaktivedanta, A.C., Swami: *Bhagvad Gītā: As It Is*: Bhaktivedanta Book Trust, Mumbai (2006 Reprint); Chapter 13.8, page 573.
7. Parthasarthy, Swami (Dr.): *Human Values and Management: 20 Key Principles for Modern Management*: Ane Books, New Delhi (2006) pp. 19-25.
10. op. cit. pp. 31-35.
11. op. cit. p. 35
14. op. cit. pp. 44-45.
15. op. cit. pp. 45-47.
17. Prabhupada, Bhaktivedanta, A.C., Swami: *Bhagvad Gītā*: *As It Is*: Bhaktivedanta Book Trust, Mumbai (2006 Reprint); Chapter 2.71, page 143.
18. Parthasarthy, Swami (Dr.): Human Values and Management: 20 Key Principles for Modern Management: Ane Books, New Delhi (2006) Pages 51-53.
19. op. cit. pp 53-56.
20. op. cit. pp. 56-60.
21. op. cit. p. 60.
22 op. cit. pp. 60-63.
23. op. cit. 63-67.
24. op. cit. pp. 67-69.
25. op. cit. pp. 69-71.
26. op. cit. pp. 71-76.
27 op. cit. pp. 76-92.

Ethical Values in Vidura Nīti

Trividhaṁ narkasyedaṁ dvāraṁ nāśanamātmanaḥ
kāmaḥ krodhastathā lobhas tasmādetattrayaṁ tyajet

'*Kāma* (Lust), *Krodha* (Anger), and *Lobha* (Greed) must be shunned by a man, as these three destroy the *Ātmā* (soul) and are the three doors to the Hell.'

(*Vidura Nīti* (VN) : Chap.1.64)

Introduction

In the literature of the whole world the historic epic *Mahābhārata* is unparallel, in which Maharṣi Veda Vyāsa declares:

dharme cārthe cakāme ca mokṣe ca puruṣarṣabha
yadihāsti tadanyatra yannehāsti na tatakvacit.

(*Mahābhārata: Ādi Parva*: 62/53)

'O the best among the Bharatas! in connection with the *Dharma* (spiritual and moral values), *Artha* (wealth), *Kāma* (worldly desire) and *Mokṣa* (liberation) whatever has been said in this book, the same is everywhere, and whatever is not narrated here, is nowhere else.'

Ancient Indian values and ethos have their basis and foundation rooted deep in *Sanātana Dharma*, which is eternal and has evolved over centuries. These eternal and ever-relevant principles focus on making the life of a common man as fruitful and relevant as possible. These principles have been imparted to the masses through various channels viz. scriptures, including *Nīti Śāstra*, etc. These ancient ethical values hold a great relevance even for modern times. *Vidura Nīti* by Mahātamā Vidura, comprising *Udyoga Parva*, sections XXXIII to XLI of *Mahābhārata*, is one of the prominent *Nitī Śāstras* containing ethical values, having relevance even today. The *Mahābhārata* is the longest epic ever written in the history of humankind. This encompasses a whole lot of knowledge in itself, as *Vidura Nīti*, *Śrimad Bhagvadgītā,* etc. are a part of this scripture only.

Mahātmā Vidura

Mahātamā Vidura is a famous character in the *Mahābhārata*, who has discussed morality in great detail in the *Vidura Nīti.* In the context of *Mahābhārata*, several *Nītis* have been compiled, among them *Nārada-Nīti* and *Vidura Nīti* are very reputed, which latter sermons delivered by high souled Mahātmā Vidura to Dhṛtrāṣṭra are the most marvellous and pertinent even today. It should have been so, because Vidura himself was a great politician, most learned and righteous person endowed with great wisdom. Vidura was one of the prominent figures in the history of the *Mahābhārata.* As per scriptures, Vidura in his previous birth was *'Dharma Deva',* the God of Justice himself. Vidura was so well up in the knowledge of *Dharma* that he was given the appellation of *'Mahātamā'* for his unparalleled knowledge of *Dharma* or righteousness and for being devoid of attachment and anger. He was fearless and truthful.

He worked as a counsellor to the king Dhṛtareṣṭra to the satisfaction of all concerned. The rulings given by him satisfied all.

Vidura respected his elder brother Dhṛtarāṣṭra, and all along he tried to guide him on the right path. During the

fratricidal war of Kurukṣetra, Vidura repeatedly implored his elder brother Dhṛtrāṣṭra to do justice to the sons of Pāṇḍu, but his son Duryodhana did not like such interference by his uncle Vidura, and rather practically insulted Vidura. Vidura was very prudent, wise, polite, religious, well- mannered and devoted to Lord Krishna. As a minister to Dhṛtarāṣṭra, he used to give him good advice. When Duryodhana was born, Vidura had cautioned him that his child would be the cause of the Kauravas' destruction, but due to the attachment for his child, Dhṛtarāṣṭra did not pay heed to his advice and as a result suffered a lot all along his life just because of Duryodhana.

Because of Duryodhana's atrocities, Mahātmā Vidura developed sympathy for the Paṇḍavas and he helped them and protected them directly or indirectly. He knew that despite any crisis, the Paṇḍavas would win the battle eventually. They were blessed with a long life and hence no one could kill them. Kunti was convinced of Vidura's words as she knew that he was a man of truth. Vidura had also cautioned Yudhiṣṭhira of the imminent danger that was lurking in *Vārṇāvata* and also told him the way to escape the danger. It was Vidura who had planned the digging of a tunnel from *Lakṣāgṛha* to the bank of the *Ganges* and had arranged for the boat to emerge on the river and finally cross it. Thus, acting prudently, Vidura saved the lives of the Pāṇḍavas. Vidura did not discriminate in his affection for the Pāṇḍavas and the Kauravas and he used to give them good advice as well. But Duryodhana never liked his advice. Even then, Vidura tried his level best to put Dhṛtarāṣṭra on the right track. But under the influence of his sons, Dhṛtarāṣ ṭra never followed Vidura's advice, although assuming him to be his well-wisher, he always sought his advice.

Following Śakuni's advice, Duryodhana informed the proposal of inviting the Pāṇḍavas over a game of dice. Vidura cautioned Dhṛtarāṣṭra that such a game would only increase the enmity between the two sides, as the game of dice was inauspicious for both the sides. Praising Vidura, Dhṛtarāṣṭra then persuaded Duryodhana to give up the plan. But Duryodhana was determined to humiliate the Pandavas, hence he made Dhṛtarāṣṭra accept his plan. Ultimately, it was Vidura who went to Indraprastha with the proposal of the game. Yudhiṣṭhira too did not like the game of dice but to honour his uncle's desire, he accepted the proposal. Even when the game was being played, Vidura tried to convince Dhṛtarāṣṭra that he still had enough time to come around and drop his submissive stance for Duryodhana and save his clan and not to make the Pāṇḍavas their enemy. Again after the Pandavas had left for exile, Dhṛtarāṣṭra was worried as to how to convince the subjects and how to please the Pāṇḍavas to return. Vidura then said: *'O King, Artha, Dharma and Kāma* (wealth, spirituality and lust) are met through *Dharma* only. *Dharma* is the pedestal of the state. Hence, you should protect yourself and the Pāṇḍavas. Your sons have snatched everything from the Pāṇḍavas. It is against the *Dharma.* Hence, you should first get Duryodhana arrested and hand over the kingdom to Yudhiṣṭhira. Yudhiṣṭhira has no envy or jealousy, hence he will rule the kingdom religiously. Ask Duśśāsana to beg for pardon from Draupadī and Bhīma in the court. Doing these things, you will be free from your worries." But Dhṛtarāṣṭra did not like this advice and he told Vidura as to how he could give up his sons just for the Pāṇḍavas sake, and ordered Vidura to leave. Anticipating the imminent fall of the Kauravas, Vidura visited Kāmyaka Vana to meet the Pāṇḍavas and told them a few things for their benefit. Dhṛtarāṣṭra having come to know of Vidura's visit to the Pāṇḍavas began to suspect that with the help of Vidura, the Pāṇḍavas would become stronger. So, he called Vidura back and begged him for pardon. At that time Vidura told Dhṛtarāṣṭra that he did not differentiate between the Kauravas and the Pāṇḍavas but seeing the Pāṇḍavas in such a hapless condition, it was but natural to help them, in any case, he did not have any partiality for the Kauravas.

Vidura was also very loyal to Lord Krishna. When Krishna came to Hastinapur with the peace proposal, he preferred to stay with Vidura relishing the plain food offered by him in contrast to the royal meal, which was being served at the palace. It is thus easy to guess the intense love of Lord Krishna for Vidura. The next day when Duryodhana tried to arrest Krishna in the palace, Vidura cautioned him and told him that Shri Krishna is the Lord Himself and any kind of disrespect for him would destroy him like a flame destroys a moth. Thereafter the Lord appeared in his cosmic form and seeing all except Vidura, Bhīṣma, Sañjay and Droṇa closed their eyes.

After the battle was over, Vidura consoled Dhṛtarāṣṭra that whoever died in the battle had attained salvation, hence one should not mourn for them. Every time a human is born, he makes new relations but after his death, these relations crumble like a castle made out of sand. Hence, it is useless to mourn for dead relatives. Events like comforts and miseries, crisis and fortune and misfortune, etc. are due to the result of one's own good or bad deeds. Every living being has to bear the fruits of his deeds. Thereafter Vidura preached the ways of observing the right conduct and how to be rid of the miseries. After the coronation of Yudhiṣṭhira, Dhṛtarāṣṭra came to stay with him. Vidura also stayed with him and used to be engaged in religious discussions. Eventually, he accompanied Dhṛtarāṣṭra, Gāndhārī and Kuntī in their penance. In the forests, observing solitude, he observed severe penance. Once Yudhiṣṭhira went to the forests to meet his mother, uncle and aunt. Not finding Vidura there, he inquired about him. At that time Vidura was heading for his hermitage far away in the jungles. Yudhiṣṭhira called out to him several times but Vidura did not pay any notice to his calls and he stood resting against a tree. Yudhiṣṭ hira hastily went near Vidura and found out that due to his severe penance, Vidura's body had been reduced to a mere skeleton. There and then, Yudhiṣṭhira worshipped him and saw a beam of light emerging from his body and merged with Yudhiṣṭhira and the lifeless body of Vidura remained resting against the tree. Thus, living a religious life, Mahātamā Vidura attained salvation.

Vidura Nīti -The Wisdom of Vidura

Nīti Śāstras are works on morals and polity, consisting either of proverbs and wise maxims in verse or of stories and fables inculcating some moral precept and illustrating its effects. These fables are generally in prose interspersed with pithy maxims in verse. Once Dhṛtarāṣṭra, who was having a sleepless night, called Vidura to seek the way for solace. The preaching which Vidura delivered during that time and subsequently, in continuation, is even today known as *Vidura Nīti.* It contains not only the fundamental principles and deep knowledge of politics, but also sermons which elevate the character of a man. The main learning out of the entire scripture is the Governance,i.e. how should an administrator run his government efficiently by following the *Dharma* and not resorting to unfair means which are not for the benefit of the stakeholders. *Mahābhārata* offers valuable lessons in international diplomacy as well as in management of public finance. In today's modern management when ethical judgment and the importance of recognizing the ethical dimensions is talked about, *Mahābhārata* gives excellent analogies to identify the ethical boundaries. "Rules of ethical conduct", *dharmayuddha* (righteous war), for the war were framed by the supreme commanders of each side. The age-old wisdom of the Indian seers seems to have caught on today in the world of management. It will only be a reclaiming of our own heritage if we in India return to our spiritual lineage and reshape it, if need be, to suit the present claims. It is apparent that we are well placed to take advantage of this knowledge economy owing to our celebrated spiritual heritage. Vidura explains codes of conduct and how one should act in different situations. His teachings are aimed at kings, ordinary citizens as well as at ascetics. For example:

➢ A king should act responsibly; otherwise, the wealth of the kingdom would be exhausted in no time.

➢ Comparing our body as a chariot, one should calmly control the horses of senses, otherwise, uncontrolled senses would lead to destruction like uncontrolled horses.

➢ As dry wood would burn wet wood, an innocent man should stay away from sinners, otherwise, he will be punished in the same way as a sinner.

Qualities of the Successful Leader

➢ Ancient Indian thinkers gave a lot of importance to leaders and leadership. A bad leader means not merely a single bad person, but a bad fate for many. In '*Vidura Nīti*' a king's basic duties are as follows:

➢ A king should wish for the prosperity of all and should

never set his heart on the misery of his subjects.

➢ A king should look after people who have fallen into adversity and who are in distress.

➢ A king should show kindness to all creatures.

➢ A king should never impede the growth and development of agriculture and economic activity in his kingdom.

➢ A king should always do that which is for the good of all creatures.

➢ A king should always be ready to protect those dependent on him.

➢ A virtuous king is never indifferent to even the minutest suffering of his subjects.

➢ A virtuous king enlists the confidence of his devoted subordinates by zealously looking after their welfare.

➢ A king who renounces lust and anger, who bestows wealth upon proper recipients, and who is discriminative, learned and active is regarded as an authority by all men.

➢ A king who desires the highest success in all matters connected with worldly profit should from the very beginning, practice virtue. Prosperity takes its birth in good deeds.

What a King Must Avoid

➢ The friendship of the sinful has to be avoided.

➢ Misuse of wealth, the harshness of speech, and extreme severity of punishment will ruin even firmly established monarchs.

➢ Evil-minded kings, due to lack of sense-control, are destroyed by lust for expanding their territory.

➢ A king's prosperity built on mere crookedness is destined to be destroyed.

➢ A king should never make a person his minister without examining him well. During the examination a king should reject those who are ungrateful, shameless, who have wicked dispositions, and who don't give others their due'.

Vidura, the learned minister of king Dhṛtarāṣṭra, has explained the most important qualities of leadership and administration. Vidura prescribes the following **values for a ruler to be a perfect leader:** simplicity, purity, contentment, truthfulness, self-restraint, patience, honesty, charity, steadiness, humility, faith, exertion, forbearance, sweetness in speech and good company.

Characteristics of Wise Persons/Mark of Wisdom:

➢ Vidura said: 'He alone is a wise man, who knows his capacity, who is never idle or lazy but exerts himself according to his might, who is not affected by pleasure or pain, profit or loss, honour or dishonour, who has a firm faith in *Dharma* and who is not tempted by sensual objects. (VN: 1.16).

➢ He, whom neither anger nor joy, nor pride, nor false modesty, nor stupefaction, nor vanity, can draw away from the high ends of life, is considered as wise. (VN: 1.18).

➢ He, whose intended acts, and proposed counsels remain concealed from foes, and whose acts become known only after they have been done, is considered wise (VN: 1.19).

➢ He, whose proposed actions are never obstructed by heat or cold, fear of attachment, prosperity or adversity, is considered wise. (VN: 1.20).

➢ He, whose worldly intelligence follows both *Dharma* (virtue) and *Artha* (wealth) and who disregarding worldly pleasures chooses *Dharma* which is serviceable in both worlds, is considered wise. (VN: 1.21).

➢ They that exert to the best of their might, and act also to the best of their might, and disregard nothing as insignificant, are called wise. (VN: 1.22).

➢ He, who grasps the most difficult subject quickly, listens to the talks of others patiently, pursues the objects of the senses with judgment and not from desire and does not give his opinion unasked, is said to possess the foremost mark of wisdom. (VN: 1.23).

➢ Those having the intelligence of a wise man, do not strive for objects that are unattainable, do not grieve for what is lost and gone, and never lose their heart (remain firm) in calamities. (VN: 1.24).

➢ He, who commences his acts with due thought and consideration, who never gives up things halfway, who never wastes his time, and who has his senses under control, is regarded wise. (VN: 1.25).

➢ They, who are wise, always delight in honest deeds, do what tends to their happiness and prosperity, and never sneer at what is good. (VN: 1.26).

➢ He, who exults not at honours, and grieves not at slights, and remains cool and unagitated like a lake in the course of *Ganga (Ganges),* is reckoned as wise. (VN: 1.27).

➢ That man who knows the nature of all creatures (viz., that everything is subject to destruction), who is cognisant also of the connections of all acts, and who is proficient in the knowledge of the means that man may resort to (for attaining their objects), is reckoned as wise. (VN: 1.28).

➢ He, who speaks eloquently, can converse on various subjects, knows the science of argumentation, possesses genius, and can interpret the hidden meaning of sacred books, is reckoned as wise. (VN: 1.29).

➢ He whose studies of the *Śāstras* (scriptures) are regulated by reason, and whose reason follows the scriptures, and who abides by the ideals or virtues of good persons and never abstains from paying respect to those that are good, is called a wise man. (VN: 1.30).

➢ He, who having attained immense wealth and prosperity or acquired (vast) learning, does not bear himself haughtily, is reckoned as wise.

The Signs of Foolish Persons

➢ He, on the other hand, who is ignorant of scriptures yet

proud, poor but builds castles in the air, and wishes to obtain things or wealth without any exertion on his part, resorts to unfair means, for the acquisition of his objects, is a fool. (VN: 1.32).

➢ He who, forsaking his own, concerns himself with the objects of others, and who is deceitful with his friends, is called a fool. (VN: 1.33).

➢ He, who wishes for those things that should not be desired, and forsakes those that may legitimately be desired, and who bears malice to those that are powerful, is regarded to be a foolish soul. (VN: 1.34).

➢ He who regards his foe as his friend, who hates and bears malice to his friend, and who commits wicked deeds, is said to be a fool. (VN: 1.35).

➢ He, who propagates his future programmes (divulges his projects), trusts none and doubts in all things, and takes a long time in doing what requires a short time, is a fool. (VN: 1.36).

➢ He, who does not assign their due share of corn, water, clothes with *Sraddha* to the *Pitṛs* (i.e. father, mother, old persons), protectors of the city and country, who does not worship the deities (i.e. who does not worship the God Almighty), who does not honour the learned and does not do good to the fire, air, water, etc., by pouring oblations in the fire, and who does not acquire noble-minded friends, is said to be a person of foolish soul. (VN: 1.37).

➢ He, who enters an assembly or another man's house uninvited, talks much without being asked, and trusts the untrustworthy or believes in what should not be believed, is verily a fool and the lowest of the low. (VN: 1.38).

➢ That man who being himself guilty casts the blame on others, and who though impotent gives vent to anger, is the most foolish among men. (VN: 1.39).

➢ That man, who without knowing his own strength desires an object, which is devoid of both virtue and profit (wealth), difficult of acquisition, without again adopting adequate means, is said to be a fool in this world. (VN: 1.40).

➢ O king, he who advises the undeserving, who keeps company with the wretched and destitute, and takes refuge in misers is said to be having little sense. (VN: 1.41).

Knowledge through numbers

The one

I. Heartless

a. Who is more **cruel and heartless** than the **one**, who, though possessed of affluence, eats alone and wears excellent robes himself, without distributing his wealth among his servants and dependents? (Obviously, none). (VN: 1.42).

2. Sin attaches to the Doer Alone

a. While **one** person commits sins (earn money by evil means), many reap the advantage resulting therefrom; (but in the end) **it is the *doer alone to whom the sin attaches,*** while those who enjoy the fruit escape unhurt. (VN: 1.43).

3. Intelligence

a. When an archer shoots an arrow, he may or may not succeed in killing even a single person, but when an intelligent individual applies his intelligence (viciously), it may destroy an entire kingdom along with the king. (VN: 1.44).

Discriminating

Discriminating the two by means of one, bring under thy subjection the three by means of four, and also conquering the five and knowing the six, and abstaining from the seven, **be happy. (VN:1.45)**

Swami Jagdishwarananda Saraswati (who recently left for heavenly abode) has explained this *Kuṭa Śloka* (a puzzling verse), as follows:

a. **One is intellect**, through which means one should *discriminate the right and wrong.*

b. Allies, neutral and foes- **these three should be brought under control** by four expedients i.e. *Sāma*, *Dāma*,

Daṇḍa and *Bheda.*

c. **Allies** should be put under control by *Sama*,- by tranquilizing words, **neutral powers** by giving something and by discrimination, and **the foe** should be brought under control by all the four expedients.

d. **By conquering the five sense organs** you should know the reality of *Sandhi* (making peace with the enemy), *Vigraha* - declaring war against the wicked enemy, *Yāna* - marching to action, *Āsana* - remaining passive, *Dvaidha (*gaining victory by dividing the forces into two), and *Samāśrya* (seeking protection of, or alliance with) a powerful king.

e. **By abstaining from seven evils** i.e. adultery, gambling (playing with dice), hunting, use of intoxicants like liquor, etc., saying unkind or hard words, infliction of a punishment without offence and spending money for sinful purposes, **be happy.**

The learned Swami has also given a **spiritual translation** of the above verse, as follows:

a. By *summum bonum* intellect one should acquire definite knowledge of soul and God.

b. Desire, anger and greed - these three should be controlled *by Sāma, dāma, Uparati and Śraddhā.*

c. By controlling five sense organs, one should be well-versed in *ṣaṭaka Sampatti* - the performance of **six kinds of acts.**

d. ***Sāma,*** restraining one's mind and soul from sins and temptations,

e. ***Dāma,*** controlling the organs of actions and living a chaste life,

f. ***Uparati***, keeping aloof from wicked persons,

g. **Titikṣā**, to be indifferent to worldly pleasures and pains, and throwing oneself heart and soul into the pursuit of the ways and means of liberation,

h. ***Śraddhā*** - to have faith in scriptures, profound scholars and men of great piety and high ideals, and

i. ***Samādhāna*** - the concentration of the mind.

The seven addictions one should abstain from are the same, as explained above.

One

a. Poison kills only **one** person who takes it, and a weapon also (kills) but one. But when secret counsels become known, *they destroy an entire kingdom with the king and the subjects.* (VN: 1.46)

b. **One** should not partake of any savoury food **alone**, *nor alone reflect in the matter of acquiring wealth or on concerns of profit*, nor alone go upon a journey, nor alone remain awake among sleeping companions. (VN: 1.47)

c. O king! Just as a boat is the only means to cross an ocean, similarly the Lord Almighty who is incomparable and **the One without a second**, is the only way to attain salvation, but you are not able to comprehend this truth. (VN: 1.48)

Forgiveness

a. There is **one only** defect in a forgiving person, and not another; that defect is that people take a forgiving person to be weak. (VN: 1.49)

b. Righteousness (*Dharma)* is the one highest good, which leads to salvation. **Forgiveness is the only supreme way to peace**; knowledge alone gives contentment and benevolence, and *Ahimsa (*non-injury) alone gives happiness. (VN: 1.50).

These Two

a. Even as a serpent devours animals living in holes, ***the earth devours these two***, viz., a king who is incompetent to fight against an invader, and a *Brāhmaṇa* (*Saṁnyasī*) who does not move from one place to another for preaching. (VN: 1.51).

b. A man can attain glory and fame in this world **by doing two things**, viz., *by refraining from harsh speech*, and by *disregarding those who are wicked.* (VN: 1.52).

c. **These two have not a will of their own**, viz., those women who covet men simply because the latter are coveted by others of their sex, and that person who regards another simply because the latter is worshipped by others. (VN: 1.53).

d. **These two are like sharp thorns afflicting the body**, viz., the desires (building castles in the air) of a poor man, and the anger of the incompetent. (VN: 1.54).

e. These two types of persons **never shine (become glorious) in this world because of their incompatible acts**, viz., a householder who is indifferent or without exertion, and a *saṁnyāsī* who is indulging in worldly affairs. (VN: 1.55).

f. O, king! these two types of persons, **live (as it were) in a region higher than the heaven** itself (i.e. they are very happy), viz., a man of power but at the same time endued with forgiveness, and a poor man who is charitable. (VN: 1.56).

g. These are only **two misuses of the wealth** which is honestly earned, viz., making gifts to the unworthy and refusing the worthy. (VN: 1.57).

h. These *two should be thrown into the water*, tightly binding weights to their necks, viz., a wealthy man that does not give away alms, and a poor man who does not exert himself and remains idle. (VN: 1.58).

i. These two, *can pierce the orb of the sun*, viz., a mendicant (*Sanyasi*) accomplished in Yoga, and a warrior who loses his life but does not run away from the battlefield. (VN: 1.59).

These Three

a. Persons well-versed in the Vedas have said that men's means of accomplishment of an object are three-fold i.e. good, middling and bad. (VN: 1.60).

b. O king, there are three kinds of men - good, indifferent and bad. They should, therefore, be **respectively employed in that kind of work for which they may be fit. (VN: 1.61).**

c. These three, O king, are *not deemed to have wealth of their own*, viz., the wife, the son and the slave, or an employee, and whatever they earn would be his to whom they belong. (VN: 1.62).

d. These three crimes shorten the life of a man, deny him of Dharma (righteousness) and bring a bad name to him viz., snatching the property of others by foul means, adultery with others' wives, and deceiving his friends. (VN: 1.63).

e. These three, besides, being destructive to one's own self, are the gates to hell, viz., lust, anger, and covetousness Men also, Therefore, the wise man should renounce them. (VN: 1.64). [Note: Compare with The *Bhagavad Gītā*, Chapter 16, verse 21. The Blessed Lord said: "Triple is the gate of this hell, destructive of the self - lust, anger and greed; therefore one should abandon these three."]

f. Verily, O Bharata, *liberating a foe from distress*, alone amounts in point of merit, to these three taken together, viz., conferring a boon, acquiring a kingdom and obtaining a son. (VN: 1.65).

g. These three refugees *should never be forsaken* even in imminent great danger, viz., an old devotee (follower), one who is serving at present and who seeks protection, saying: 'I am thine'. (VN: 1.66).

These Four

a. Learned men have declared that even **a king, although powerful, should never consult with these four,** viz., men of small sense (foolish persons), men that are procrastinating (slow in action), men that are enthusiastic or who are thoughtless, and men that are flatterers. (VN: 1.67).

b. O sire, *crowned with prosperity and leading the life of a householder, let these four dwell with thee,* viz., old consanguineous relatives, high-born persons fallen into adversity, poor friends, and issueless sisters. (VN: 1.68).

c. On being asked by the chief of the celestials Indra, Vrihaspati, O mighty king, declared **four things capable of**

fructifying or occurring immediately, within a single day, viz., the resolve of the gods, the influence of the intelligent persons, the humility of learned men, and the renunciation of evil habits or destruction of the sinful. (VN: 1.69-70).

d. **These four that are performed to remove fear, *bring on fear when they are improperly performed,*** viz., the ***Agnihotra*** (sacred fire ceremony of pouring oblations in the fire), in accordance with the scriptures**, the vow of silence** according to Sastras, **study in accordance with scriptures** and ***Yajña*** (i.e. any good deed performed for the benefit of the Society). (VN: 1.71).

It may be added that *Agnihotra*, etc., when performed according to *Śāstras* bear good results but when they are performed with vanity or conceit they become harmful.

These Five

a. **These five fires should be worshipped with regard by a person**, viz., father, mother, *Agni-hotra* fire (proper), soul, and preceptor. (VN: 1.72).

b. **By serving these five kinds of persons, men attain great fame and glory** in this world, i.e. ***Deva*** *(learned persons)*, ***the Pitṛs*** (father, mother, teacher and the like), ***Manuṣya*** (old persons, lepers, beggars,etc.) and ***Atithi*** (guests- who come by chance). (VN: 1.73).

c. These five follow thee wherever you go, viz., friends, foes, those that are indifferent, dependants, and those who want refuge and are entitled to maintenance. (VN: 1.74).

d. Out of the five sense organs (eyes, ears, nose, tongue, skin) of a man, if one springs a leak, then from that single hole runs out all his intelligence, just like water runs out from a perforated leathern vessel. (VN: 1.75).

These Six

1. These **six faults should be avoided** by a person who wishes to attain prosperity and happiness, viz., sleep, drowsiness, fear, anger, laziness and procrastination. (VN:

1.76).

2. Verily those **six qualities should never be forsaken by men**, viz., truth, charity, diligence, benevolence, forgiveness and patience. (VN: 1.77).

3. **These six should be renounced** like a broken boat in the sea, viz. a preceptor who cannot expound the scriptures (who cannot teach), a priest who is illiterate, a king who is unable to defend, a wife who is disloyal, a cow-herd who does not want to go to the fields, instead who wishes to remain in the village, and a barber who wishes to live in the woods instead of a village. (VN: 1.78-79).

4. O king! **these six comprise the happiness of men**, viz. acquirement of wealth, uninterrupted sound health, agog-looking and beloved wife with sweet speech, an obedient son and knowledge that is lucrative or the knowledge which is learnt by knowing its meaning. (VN: 1.80).

5. O king! Sound health, debtlessness (being debt-free), living at home (not living in foreign lands), companionship with good men, certainty as regards the means of livelihood, and living without fear- these six **conduce to the happiness of men. (VN: 1.81).**

6. He who brings under his control these six - lust, anger, sorrow, attachment, vanity and self-conceit, which are always present in the human heart, and thus becomes the master of his senses, never commits sins and, therefore, can never suffer from calamities. (VN: 1.82).

7. The following six may be seen to subsist upon the other six, and there is no seventh who depends on some other. These are: thieves upon persons who are careless, physicians on persons who are ailing, prostitutes upon persons suffering from lust, the priests upon their Yajmanas (the institutor of a sacrifice(who pour oblations in the fire), a king upon persons that quarrel and lastly men of learning upon them who are without it. (VN: 1.83-84).

8. **These six are instantly destroyed if neglected**, viz., kine (cow), services (the work which is under the supervision

of servants), agriculture, a wife, learning, and the company of a base person. (VN: 1.85).

9. **These six forget those who have bestowed obligations on them**, viz., educated disciples, their preceptors; married persons, their mothers; persons whose desires have been gratified, women; they who have achieved success, they who had rendered aid; they who have crossed a river, the boat (that carried them over); and patients that have been cured, (forget) their physicians. (VN: 1.86-87).

10. **These six are always miserable,** viz., the envious, the malicious, the discontented, the irascible, the ever-suspicious and those depending upon the fortunes of others. (VN: 1.88).

These Seven

1. **A king should renounce these seven faults** which are productive of calamity, inasmuch as they are able to effect the ruin of even monarchs firmly established; these are *women, dice, hunting, drinking, the harshness of speech, severity of punishment, and misuse of wealth.* (*VN:* 1.89-90).

These Eight

1. **These eight are the immediate indications of a man destined to destruction**, viz., hating the Brāhmaṇas (scholars), dispute with Brāhmaṇas, appropriation of a Brāhmaṇa's possessions, taking the life of a Brāhmaṇa, taking a pleasure in reviling Brāhmaṇas, grieving to hear the praises of Brahmanas, forgetting them on ceremonious occasions, and giving vent to spite when they ask for anything. These transgressions a wise man should understand and understanding, renounce them. (VN: 1.91-93).

2. These eight, O Bharata, **are the very cream of happiness, and these are the only means of prosperity in this world**, viz., meeting with friends, accession of immense wealth, embracing a son, full satisfaction of husband and wife after intercourse, speaking sweet words at the right occasion or conversation with friends at proper times, advancement in one's own class or party, the acquisition of what was most

cherished and respect in the society. (VN: 1.94-96).

3. These **eight qualities glorify a man**, viz., wisdom, high birth, self-restraint, learning, prowess, moderation in speech, gift according to one's power, and gratitude.

These Nine

1. This house has nine doors (i.e. two eyes, two ears, two holes of the nostril, one mouth, the holes of anus and penis), three pillars) *Sattva, Rajas and Tamas* - goodness, passion and darkness or virtue, foulness and ignorance), and five witnesses (sound, tangibility, shape or colour, flavour and smell). It is presided over by the soul. The learned man who knows the abode of the soul - the human body, with these nine gates, three pillars and five witnesses, is truly a wise man. (VN: 1.97).

These Ten

1. O Dhṛtareṣṭra, **these ten do not know what Dharma (virtue) is**, viz., the intoxicated, inattentive, the mad (raving), the fatigued, the angry, the hungry, the hasty, the covetous, the frightened, and the lustful. Therefore, he, who is wise, should not keep company with them (VN: 1.98-99).

2. **The king who renounces lust and anger**, who bestows wealth upon proper recipients, and who is discriminating, learned, and active, is regarded as an authority by all men. (VN: 1.101)

3. Great prosperity attends upon that king who knows how to inspire confidence in others, who inflicts punishment on those whose guilt has been proved, who is acquainted with the proper measure of punishment, and who knows when mercy is to be shown. (VN: 1.102).

4. **He is a self-possessed person** who does not disregard even a very weak and humble person, who proceeds with intelligence and care in respect of a foe, who is anxiously watching for an opportunity, who does not desire hostilities with persons stronger than himself, and who displays his prowess at the proper time. (VN: 1.103).

5. **That illustrious person**, who does not grieve when a calamity befalls on him, who exerts with all his collected senses, and who patiently bears misery in distress, is really the foremost of persons, and all his foes are already vanquished. (VN: 1.104)

6. He who does not live away from home uselessly, who does not make friends with sinful persons, who never indulges with another's wife, who never betrays, and who never commits a theft, who neither backbites nor indulges in drinking or shows ingratitude **is always happy**. (VN: 1.105).

7. He who never boastfully strives to attain the three objects of human pursuit, viz. *Dharma* (virtue), *Artha* (wealth) and *Kama* (desire), who when asked, tells the truth, who does not quarrel over trifles even for the sake of friends, and who never becomes angry though slighted, **is reckoned as wise**. (VN: 1.106).

8. He, who neither bears malice towards others nor becomes angry, but is kind to all, who being weak never quarrels with others or does not stand surety for anyone, who does not speak arrogantly, and avoids controversy**, is praised everywhere**. (VN: 1.107).

9. That man who never assumes a haughty mien, who does not boast of his valour in the presence of others, agitated even by anger, never speaks harsh words - **is ever loved by all.** (VN: 1.108).

10. He who rakes not up to old hostilities, who behaves neither arrogantly nor with too much humility, 'I am in distress' - saying so who does not commit improper acts, is considered by respectable men as a **person of good conduct - a nobleman.** (VN: 1.109).

11. He, who never exults at his own happiness, nor delights in another's misery, and who repents not after giving charity, is said to be a man of **good nature and conduct**. (VN: 1.110).

12. He, who has a knowledge of the customs of different

countries, and also the rules and languages of different nations, and usages of different orders of men, is a discreet person - he **knows at once all that is high and low**. Wherever he may go, he is sure to gain sway/ascendancy over the public and rules them. He is respected and adored by all. (VN: 1.111).

13. The prudent/ **intelligent person** who **relinquishes** hypocracy (performing of religious ceremony in order to cheat the public), folly, jealousy, sinful acts, disloyalty towards the king, crookedness of behaviour, enmity with many, and also not quarrels with men that are drunk, mad and wicked, **is the foremost of his species**. (VN: 1.112).

14. **The very gods - the learned men and divine powers bestow prosperity upon him** and lead him towards excellence, who does the following deeds daily- viz. gives charity, purifies himself inwardly and outwardly, performs *Agni-hotra*, performs auspicious rites, repents for his bad deeds, and performs rites of universal observance practises self-restraint, purification, auspicious rites, worship of the gods, expiatory ceremonies, and other rites of universal observance. (VN: 1.113).

15. The policies of that learned man are well-conceived and well-applied (are successful), who forms matrimonial alliances with persons of equal position and not with those that are inferior, who talks and talks, behaves and makes friendships with persons of equal position, places those before him who are more qualified - thinks them as ideal. (VN: 1.114).

16. The calamities and sufferings always keep themselves aloof from that person, who has soul under his control- who is determined, who eats frugally after dividing the food amongst his dependents, uses the clothing, etc. in small quantity, who sleeps little after working much, and who, when asked gives away even unto his foes. (VN: 1.115).

17. The man whose well-planned and spoiled works are never known to others, whose counsels are well-kept and become known to others only when they are carried out into practice, his works are never spoiled - he succeeds in all his objects. (VN: 1.116).

18. He who is intent upon abstaining from injury to all creatures, who is truthful, tender-hearted, who respects others and pure in mind, shines greatly among his kinsmen like a precious gem of the purest ray having its origin in an excellent mine. (VN: 1.117).

19. That man, who without being told by another, himself knowing his fault, feels ashamed, becomes the preceptor of the whole world - he is highly honoured among all men. He, who is possessed of immense luster, cheerful mind, pure heart and a steady intellect, shines with energy like the very Sun. (VN: 1.118).

Conclusion

From the perusal of the above advice given by Mahātamā Vidura to king Dhṛtarāṣṭra, it will be observed that many gems of ethical values are contained in the Vidura Nīti, which are still relevant in modern times. Commencing from *'to whom sleep evades'*, *'the characteristic of wise men'* and the *'traits of foolish persons'*, Vidura has spread a wide spectrum of variegated rules of conduct, which though meant for Dhṛtarāṣṭ ra, are relevant to all of us even in the present times, when the degradation of ethical values has become rampant all around the world. Let us ponder over some of them to be more wise, prudent, and successful in the ultimate reckoning.

References

1. *Vidura Nīti* (Trilingual- Sanskrit, Hindi, and English) by Pramahansa Swami Jagdishwarananda: Vijay Kumar Govindram Hasanand, Delhi (2005).
2. *The Mahābhārata: Udyoga Parva,* Sections XXXIII to XLI; Translated by Sri Kisari Mohan Ganguli.
3. *Maxims of Vidura*: G.N.Das: Abhinav Publications, Delhi(1987).

Panoramic View of Ethical Values from Chāṇakya's Nītiśāstra

Although many great savants of the science of *niti* such as Bṛhaspati, Śukrācārya (*Śukra Nīti*), Vidur (*Vidur Nīti),* Bhartṛhari (*Bhartṛhari Śataka*) and Viṣṇu Śarmā have echoed many of ethical instructions and cherished values in the shape of *nītis* or instructions in their own celebrated works, it is perhaps the way that Chāṇakya applied his teachings of *Nīti-Śāstra* that has made him stand out as a significant historical figure. He teaches us that *how lofty ideals can become a certain reality if we intelligently work towards achieving our goal in a determined, progressive and practical manner.* In Chāṇakya's *Nīti Śāstra* we see many subtleties of his vast wit and wisdom. The real goal of *Nīti,* indeed the goal of life, is to realise one's eternal position, but certain guidelines for leading the social life in the worldly existence smoothly are also necessary in the present times. Learned Chāṇakya comes to our rescue in this regard with certain maxims, through his monumental work 'Cāṇakya *Nīti Śāstra*'(CNS), which may still be found relevant to face the emerging situations in the so-called '*Kaliyuga*' Moreover, there is a need to have a relevant presentation and re-look at some of the ancient works like this *Nīti-Śāstra* (scripture), for being applied effectively in the context of modern times.

We rarely come across some great men and legendary characters, who shaped time through their vision and exemplary actions. Chāṇakya, perhaps is the only personality who has been accepted and revered as a genius both by Indian and Western scholars. *He is a historical milestone in the making of India* amidst tremendous upheavals and myriad's of reversals. Celebrated as a shrewd statesman and a ruthless administrator, he comes across as the greatest of diplomats of the world. He had the guts to speak his heart out even in front of the rulers, which shows his strong inclination to democratic values and the audacity to put his views through. Although he lived centuries before, his ideas and principles show concurrence and validity even in the present-day world. Politics was his forte. Diplomacy in the then politically charged environment shows his self-confidence and the ability to stay calm in trying situations. His foresight and wide knowledge coupled with politics of expediency founded the mighty Mauryan Empire in India.

At a very early age, little Chāṇakya started studying Vedas. The Vedas, considered to be the toughest scriptures to study, were completely studied and memorized by Chāṇakya in his infancy. He was attracted to studies in politics. In politics, Chāṇakya's acumen and shrewdness was visible right from childhood. Known as a masterful political strategist, he knew how to put his own people in the opposite camp and spy on the enemy without his knowledge before destroying him forever. Chāṇakya was an ace in turning tables in his favour irrespective of the circumstances. He never budged to pressure tactics by the ruthless politicians. In this way after studying religion and politics, he turned his attention to economics, which remained his lifelong friend. Takshashila, (Taxila), one of the topmost centres of education at that time in India, became Chāṇakya's breeding ground for acquiring knowledge in the practical and theoretical aspects. The university at Taxila was well- versed in teaching the subjects using the best of practical knowledge acquired by the teachers. The branches of studies most sought after in and around India ranged from law, medicine, warfare and other indigenous forms of learning. The four Vedas, archery, hunting, elephant-lore and 18 arts were taught at the university. After acquiring vast knowledge in various branches of study he wanted everybody to get benefited. He believed in the broadcasting of knowledge and not in the storage of it. The whole nation was bewildered by the cleverness and wit of this seemingly small boy who went on to single-handedly to unify the country with the sheer power of his character. *He lived his life working to his capacity in pursuit of his vision of a happy strong and prosperous India.* Thus, through his conscientious efforts, the indigenous Vedic culture of the sacred land of Bharata (India) was protected and the spiritual practices of the Hindus could go on unhampered.

He was also a great laureate of economics with a glittering intellect to perceive the intricate dynamics of the various economic activities and principles, which he espoused through his masterpiece '*Arthaśāstra*'. The centuries that succeeded him show distinct effects of his thoughts on the way a kingdom should be managed and other facets of economic administration. Even today, one of his maxims on taxation is very much alive and calls for adherence by the governments of the world. According to Chāṇakya, '*Taxation should not be a painful process for the people. There should be leniency and caution while deciding the tax structure. Ideally, governments should collect taxes like a honeybee, which sucks just the right amount of honey from the flower so that both can survive. Taxes should be collected in small and not in large proportions*'. His contribution to foreign policy in the present-day world is immense. Universities teach his principles to aspiring foreign policy experts showing the infallibility of his principles. Chāṇakya's art of diplomacy is well known across India and practised in the areas of defence, strategy formation and foreign relations. Quite remarkably, long before Clausewitz came up with the quote, which said '*War is only the continuance of state policy by other means*', Chāṇakya had already written it in his book '*Chāṇakyanīti*'. Most of his views were so farsighted that they appeared to be prophesies. Talking on diverse subjects such as corruption, he commented very rightly, *'It's just as difficult to detect an official's dishonesty as it is to discover how much water is drunk by the swimming fish'*.

As a person, Chāṇakya has been described variously, as a saint, as a 'ruthless administrator', as the 'kingmaker', a devoted nationalist, a selfless ascetic, and even by some as a person devoid of all morals. He created controversy by saying '*The ends justify the means' and the ruler should use any means to attain his goals and his actions required no moral sanctions.* All his written works namely, '*Arthaśāstra*',

'*Nītiśāstra*' and '*Chāṇakyanīti*' were unique because of their rational approach and an unabashed advocacy of real politic. His views were dimensionally novel. He recommended even espionage and the liberal use of provocative agents as machineries of the state. In politics, he even attested to 00the use of false accusations and killings by a king's secret agent without any ambiguities. In his view, the observance of morals and ethics was secondary to the interests of the ruler. Some of his stark views made him into an ambivalent personality for the world. This great statesman and philosopher has been often compared to Machiavelli, Aristotle and Plato, exemplifying his potentiality and influential status. He has been criticised for his ruthlessness and trickery and praised for his profound political wisdom. Chāṇakya, the timeless man, was in pursuit of truth fearlessly over 2000 years ago and was proved right with Vivekanand's words, '*Arise, Awake, Sleep not till the goal is reached*'.

Chāṇakya envisioned India as a nation which would place itself as the forerunner - politically, economically and socially. His magnum opus, '*Arthaśāstra*', depicts in many ways the India of His dreams. When he wrote this volume of epic proportion, the country was ridden in feudalism and self-sufficient economy based on indigenous ways of production; was in a transitional phase, moving towards the advanced aspects of distribution and production. Culture and regional politics directed the way in which trade was done. The main activities of the economy were agriculture, cattle rearing and commerce. Among the three, Chāṇakya considered agriculture to be the most important constituent of the economy. Covering various topics on administration, politics and economy, it is a book of law and a treatise on running a country which is relevant even today. People who think that the society in which we live will remain the same; are dissuading themselves of the truth. Society is a complex and dynamic system changing constantly leaving those people behind who say 'no' to change.

Broadly speaking, Chāṇakya dreamt of a country reaching the following levels of development in terms of ideologies and social and economic development:

* A self- sufficient economy, an egalitarian society with equal opportunities for all, development of natural and man-made resources, efficient management of land for the development of resources, and the state keeping an eye on the occupation of excess land by the landlords and unauthorised use of land, and ideally the state should monitor the most important and vital resource of Land. The state should take care of agriculture at all times. Government machinery should be directed towards the implementation of projects aimed at supporting and nurturing the various processes; beginning from the sowing of seeds to harvest.

* Internal trade was more important to Chāṇakya than external trade. At each point of the entry of goods, a minimal amount of tax should be collected. The state should collect taxes at a bare minimum level, so that there is no chance of tax evasion.

* The laws of the state should be the same for all, irrespective of the person who is involved in the case. Destitute women should be protected by society because they are the result of social exploitation and the uncouth behaviour of men.

* Security of the citizens at peacetime is very important because the state is the only saviour of the men and women who get affected only because of the negligence of the state. Anti-social elements should be kept under check along with the spies who may enter the country at any time.

Chāṇakya, apart from being a man of wisdom and unfailing strategies, propounded *Nītiśāstra,* in which he espoused the ideal way of living for every individual of the society. By writing '*Arthaśāstra*' and '*Nītiśāstra*, Chāṇakya has become a never-ending phenomenon. His '*Nītiśāstra*', a treatise on the ideal way of life, shows his in-depth study of the Indian way of life. In his epoch-making *Chāṇakya Nīti Śāstra* (CNS), he also envisioned a society where the people are not running behind material pleasures. Control over the sense organs is essential for success in any endeavour. Spiritual development is essential for the internal strength and character of the individual. Material pleasures and achievements are always secondary to the spiritual development of the society and country at large.

He has truly guided the generations with his wisdom.

The moral values envisaged in the Chāṇakya's '*Nīti Śāstra*' are one of the best-known Nīti Śāstras on religious and social obligations.

Let us have a panoramic view of the ethical concepts in Chāṇakya's *Nīti Śāstra* (CNS) to adjudge whether some of them are akin or a bit different to the Vedic ethics and values and to consider their relevance to the present times. However, we need to judge the CNS in the light of present times. In the words of Will Durant 'the historian's folly is to judge the past from the yardstick of the present', and we should accord CNS due to scholarly sensitivity, concern and understanding. In the very first few verses (CNS: 2-3) the learned Chāṇakya states that he is reciting these maxims of the science of political ethics (*Nīti*) selected from the various *Śāstras* with an eye to the public good. He further asserts that the man who by the study of these maxims from the *Śāstras* acquires a knowledge of the most celebrated principles of duty, and understands what ought and what ought not to be followed, and what is good and what is bad, is most excellent.

Vedic Lore

* Do not stay for a single day where there are not these five persons: a wealthy man, a scholar well-versed in Vedic lore, a king, a river, and a physician. (CNS:1.9)

* Let not a single day pass without your learning a verse, half a verse, or a fourth of it, or even one letter of it; nor without attending to charity, study, and other pious activity. (CNS: 2.13).

* Those who blaspheme Vedic wisdom, who ridicule the lifestyle recommended in the *Śāstras* (scriptures), and who deride men of peaceful temperament, come to grief unnecessarily. (CNS: 5.10).

* Chanting of the Vedas without performing *yajñas*, followed by their proper knowledge is futile. Perfection can be achieved only through devotion, for devotion is the basis of all success. (CNS: 8.10).

* Of those who have studied the Vedas for material

rewards---what potency have they? They are just like serpents without fangs. (CNS: 9.8)

* The house in which the lotus feet of scholars are not washed, in which Vedic mantras are not loudly recited, and in which the *Yajñas* and *Svadhā* (offerings to the elderly persons and living beings around us) are not performed, is like a crematorium. (CNS: 2.10).

* One may know the four Vedas and the *Dharma-śāstras*, yet if he has no realisation of the Supreme self, he can be said to be like the ladle which stirs all kinds of foods but knows not the taste of any. (CNS: 5.12).

On Saintly Men/Spiritual Merit

* One should save his money against hard times, save his wife with the help of his riches, but invariably one should save his soul even with the help of his wife and riches. (CNS:1.6).

* He, who gives up what is imperishable for that which perishable, loses that which is imperishable; and doubtlessly loses that which is perishable also. (CNS: 1.13)

* To have the ability for eating when dishes are ready at hand, to be robust and virile in the company of one's religiously wedded wife, and to have a mind for making charity when one is prosperous are the fruits of no ordinary austerities. (CNS:2.2).

* At the time of the *pralaya* (universal destruction), the oceans are to exceed their limits and seek to change, but a saintly man never changes. (CNS: 3.6).

* The beauty of a cuckoo is in its notes, that of a woman in her unalloyed devotion to her husband, that of an ugly person in his scholarship, and that of an ascetic in his forgiveness. (CNS: 3.9).

* There is no poverty for the industrious. Sin does not attach itself to the person practising *japa* (chanting of the holy names of the Lord). Those who are absorbed in *maunam* (silent contemplation of the Lord) have no quarrel with others. They are fearless who remain always alert. (CNS: 3.11).

* He who has not acquired one of the following: religious merit (*dharma*), wealth (*artha*), satisfaction of desires (*kāma*), or liberation (*mokṣa*) is repeatedly born to die. (CNS: 3.20).

* Offspring, friends and relatives flee from a devotee of the Lord: yet those who follow him bring merit to their families through their devotion. (CNS:4.2)

* Fish, tortoises, and birds bring up their young by means of sight, attention and touch; so do saintly men afford protection to their associates by the same means. (CNS:4.3)

* As long as your body is healthy and under control and death is distant, try to save your soul; when death is immanent what can you do? (CNS:4.4).

* Religious austerities should be practised alone, study by two, and singing by three. A journey should be undertaken by four, agriculture by five, and war by many together (CNS: 4.12).

* For the student, the teacher (Agni) is a representative of God. The Supreme Lord resides in the heart of His devotees. Those of average intelligence (*alpa-buddhi* or *kaniṣṭ ha-adhikārī*) see God only in His *Śri-murti*, but those of broad vision see the Supreme Lord everywhere. (CNS: 4.19).

* A man is born alone and dies alone; and he experiences the good and bad consequences of his *karma* alone; and he goes alone to hell or the Supreme abode. (CNS: 5.13).

* Heaven is but a straw to him who knows spiritual life; so is life to a valiant man; a woman to him who has subdued his senses; and the universe to him who is without attachment for the world. (CNS: 5.14).

* The poor wish for wealth; animals for the faculty of speech; men wish for heaven; and godly persons for liberation. (CNS: 5.18).

* The earth is supported by the power of truth; it is the power of truth that makes the sun shine and the winds blow; indeed all things rest upon truth. (CNS: 5.19).

* The Goddess of wealth is unsteady (*cañcala*), and so is the life-breath. The duration of life is uncertain, and the place

of habitation is uncertain; but in all this inconsistent world religious merit alone is immovable. (CNS: 5.20).

* By means of hearing one understands *dharma*, malignity vanishes, knowledge is acquired, and liberation from material bondage is gained. (CNS: 6.1).

* Those born blind cannot see; similarly blind are those in the grip of lust. Proud men have no perception of evil; and those bent on acquiring riches see no sin in their actions. (CNS: 6.8).

* The spirit soul goes through his own course of *karma* and he himself suffers the good and bad results thereby accrued. By his own actions he entangles himself in *sansāra*, and by his own efforts, he extricates himself. (CNS: 6.9).

* The following four characteristics of the denizens of heaven may be seen in the residents of this earth planet; charity, sweet words, worship of the Supreme Personality of Godhead, and satisfying the needs of scholars. (CNS: 7.16).

* The following qualities of the denizens of hell may characterise men on earth; extreme wrath, harsh speech, enmity with one's relations, the company with the base, and service to men of low extraction. (CNS: 7.17).

* As you seek fragrance in a flower, oil in the sesamum seed, fire in wood, ghee in milk, and jaggery (*guḍa*) in sugarcane; so seek the spirit that is in the body by means of discrimination. (CNS: 7.21).

* My dear child, if you desire to be free from the cycle of birth and death, then abandon the objects of sense gratification as poison. Drink instead the nectar of forbearance, upright conduct, mercy, cleanliness and truth. (CNS: 9.1).

* We should carefully scrutinise that place upon which we step (having it ascertained to be free from filth and living creatures like insects, etc.); we should drink water which has been filtered; we should speak only those words which have the sanction of the *Śāstras*; and do that act which we have carefully considered. (CNS: 10.2).

* He who desires sense gratification must give up all thoughts of acquiring knowledge; and he who seeks knowledge

must not hope for sense gratification. How can he who seeks sense gratification acquire knowledge, and he who possesses knowledge to enjoy mundane sense pleasure? (CNS: 10.3)

* What good can the scriptures do to a man who has no sense of his own? Of what use is a mirror to a blind man? (CNS: 10.9).

* (Through the night) a great many kinds of birds perch on a tree but in the morning they fly in all the ten directions. Why should we lament for that? (Similarly, we should not grieve when we must inevitably part company from our dear ones). (CNS: 10.15).

* (It is said that a *Sādhu*, when asked about his family, replied thus: truth is my mother, and my father is spiritual knowledge; righteous conduct is my brother, and mercy is my friend, inner peace is my wife, and forgiveness is my son: these six are my kinsmen. (CNS: 12.11).

* Our bodies are perishable, wealth is not at all permanent and death is always nearby. Therefore, we must immediately engage in acts of merit. (CNS: 12.12).

* He who regards another's wife as his mother, the wealth that does not belong to him as a lump of mud, and the pleasure and pain of all other living beings as his own -- truly sees things in the right perspective, and he is a true Paṇḍit (learned person). (CNS: 12.14).

* Rāghava, the love of virtue, pleasing speech, and an ardent desire for performing acts of charity, guileless dealings with friends, humility in the guru's presence, deep tranquillity of mind, pure conduct, discernment of virtues, realised knowledge of the *Śāstras*, beauty of form and devotion to God are all found in you. (The great sage Vasiṣṭha Muni, the spiritual preceptor of Śri Rāmacandra said this at the time of His proposed coronation). (CNS: 12.15). The desire tree is wood; the golden Mount Meru is motionless; the wish-fulfilling gem *cintāmaṇi* is just a stone; the sun is scorching; the moon is prone to wane; the boundless ocean is saline; the demigod of lust lost his body (due to Śiva's wrath); Bali Maharaja, the son of Diti, was born into a clan of demons; and Kāmadhenu (the cow of heaven) is a mere beast. O Lord of the Raghu dynasty!

I cannot compare you to any one of these (taking their merits into account). (CNS: 12.16).

* A man may live but for a moment, but that moment should be spent in doing auspicious deeds. It is useless living even for a Kalpa (43,20,000 X 1000 years) and bringing only distress upon the two worlds (this world and the next). (CNS: 13.1).

* I consider him who does not act religiously as dead though living, but he who dies acting religiously unquestionably lives long though he is dead. (CNS: 13.9).

* He who has acquired neither virtue, wealth, satisfaction of desires nor salvation (*dharma*, *artha*, *kāma*, *mokṣa*), lives an utterly useless life, like the 'nipples' hanging from the neck of a goat. (CNS: 13.10).

* Excessive attachment to sense pleasures leads to bondage, and detachment from sense pleasures leads to liberation; therefore, it is the mind alone that is responsible for bondage or liberation. (CNS: 13.12).

* He who sheds bodily identification by means of knowledge of the indwelling Supreme Self (*Paramātmā*), will always be absorbed in meditative trance (*samādhi*) wherever his mind leads him. (CNS: 13.13).

* As a calf follows its mother among a thousand cows, so the (good or bad) deeds of a man follow him. (CNS: 13.15).

* Men reap the fruits of their deeds, and intellects bear the mark of deeds performed in previous lives; even so the wise act after due circumspection. (CNS: 13.18).

* Even the man who has taught the spiritual significance of just one letter ought to be worshipped. (CNS: 13.19).

* At the end of the *Yuga*, Mount Meru may be shaken; at the end of the *Kalpa*, the waters of the seven oceans may be disturbed; but a *Sādhu* will never swerve from the spiritual path. (CNS: 13.20).

* We should not feel pride in our charity, austerity, valour, scriptural knowledge, modesty and morality, for the world is full of the rarest gems. (CNS: 14.7).

* He should be considered to be living, who is virtuous and pious, but the life of a man who is destitute of religion and virtues is void of any blessing. (CNS: 14.12).

* If you wish to gain control of the world by the performance of a single deed, then keep the following fifteen, which are prone to wander here and there, from getting the upper hand of you: the five sense objects (objects of sight, sound, smell, taste, and touch); the five sense organs (ears, eyes, nose, tongue and skin) and the (five) organs of activity (hands, legs, mouth, genitals and anus). (CNS: 14.13).

* Śāstric knowledge is unlimited, and the arts to be learned are many; the time we have is short, and our opportunities to learn are beset with obstacles. Therefore, select for learning that which is most important, just as the swan drinks only the milk in water. (CNS: 15.10)

* There are two nectar like fruits hanging from the tree of this world: one is the hearing of sweet words and the other, the society of saintly men. (CNS: 16.18).

* The good habits of charity, learning and austerity practised during many past lives continue to be cultivated in this birth by virtue of the link (*yoga*) of this present life to the previous ones. (CNS: 16.19).

* That thing which is distant, that thing which appears impossible, and that which is far beyond our reach, can be easily attained through *tapasyā* (religious austerity), for nothing can surpass austerity. (CNS: 17.3).

* What vice could be worse than covetousness? What is more sinful than slander? For one who is truthful, what need is there for austerity? For one who has a clean heart, what is the need for pilgrimage? If one has a good disposition, what other virtue is needed? If a man has fame, what is the value of other ornamentation? What need is there for wealth for the man of practical knowledge? And if a man is dishonoured, what could there be worse in death? (CNS: 17.4).

* Though the sea, which is the reservoir of all jewels, is the father of the conch shell, and the Goddess of fortune Lakshmi is conch's sister, still the conch must go from door to

door for alms (in the hands of a beggar). It is true, therefore, that one gains nothing without having given in the past. (CNS: 17.5).

* When a man has no strength left in him he becomes a *Sādhu*, one without wealth acts like a *Brahmacārī*, a sick man behaves like a devotee of the Lord, and when a woman grows old she becomes devoted to her husband. (CNS: 17.6).

* He who nurtures benevolence for all creatures within his heart overcomes all difficulties and will be the recipient of all types of riches at every step. (CNS: 17.15).

Wealth

- Save your wealth against future calamity. Do not say, 'What fear has a rich man of calamity?' When riches begin to forsake one even the accumulated stock dwindles away. (CNS: 1.7)

- Lakshmi, the Goddess of wealth, comes of Her own accord where fools are not respected, the grain is well stored up, and the husband and wife do not quarrel. (CNS: 3.21).

- He who has wealth has friends. He who is wealthy has relatives. The rich one alone is called a man, and the affluent alone are respected as Paṇḍits (learned person) (CNS: 6.5).

- Accumulated wealth is saved by spending just as incoming fresh water is saved by letting out stagnant water. (CNS: 7.14).

- Low-class men desire wealth; middle class men both wealth and respect; but the noble honour only; hence honour is the noble man's true wealth. (CNS: 8.1)

- Wise man! Give your wealth only to the worthy and never to others. The water of the sea received by the clouds is always sweet. The rainwater enlivens all living beings of the earth both movable (insects, animals, humans, etc.) and immovable (plants, trees, etc.), and then returns to the ocean, its value multiplied a million fold. (CNS: 8.4).

- The meritorious should give away in charity all that they have in excess of their needs. By charity, only Karna, Bali and King Vikramaditya survive even today. Just see the plight of the honeybees beating their legs in despair upon the earth. They are saying to themselves, 'Alas! We neither enjoyed our stored-up honey nor gave it in charity, and now someone has taken it from us in an instant.' (CNS: 11.18)

- He, who is not shy in the acquisition of wealth, grain and knowledge, and in taking his meals, will be happy. (CNS: 12.21).

- As centesimal droppings will fill a pot so also are knowledge, virtue and wealth gradually obtained. (CNS: 12.22).

- See what a wonder it is! The doings of the great are strange: they treat wealth as light as a straw, yet, when they obtain it, they bend under its weight. (CNS: 13.5)

- He who loses his money is forsaken by his friends, his wife, his servants and his relations; yet when he regains his riches those who have forsaken him come back to him. Hence, wealth is certainly the best of relations. (CNS: 15.5)

- Sinfully acquired wealth may remain for ten years; in the eleventh year, it disappears with even the original stock. (CNS: 15.6).

- I do not deserve that wealth which is to be attained by enduring much suffering, or by transgressing the rules of virtue, or by flattering an enemy. (CNS: 16.11)

- Those who were not satiated with the enjoyment of wealth, food and women have all passed away; there are others now passing away who have likewise remained unsatiated; and in the future still, others will pass away feeling themselves unsatiated. (CNS: 16.13).

Learning / Learned Person

- Even a learned person comes to grief by giving instruction to a foolish disciple, by maintaining a wicked wife, and by excessive familiarity with the miserable. (CNS: 1.4).

- Learning is like a cow of desire. It, like her, yields in all seasons. Like a mother, it feeds you on your journey. Therefore, learning is a hidden treasure. (CNS: 4.5)

- The learned are envied by the foolish; rich men by the poor; chaste women by adulteresses; and beautiful ladies by ugly ones. (CNS: 5.6)

- Learning is retained through putting into practice; family prestige is maintained through good behaviour; a respectable person is recognised by his excellent qualities; and anger is seen in the eyes. (CNS: 5.8).

- Of what avail is a high birth if a person is destitute of scholarship? A man who is of low extraction is honoured even by the demigods if he is learned. (CNS:8.19)

- A learned man is honoured by the people. A learned man commands respect everywhere for his learning. Indeed, learning is honoured everywhere. (CNS: 8.20).

- Those who are endowed with beauty and youth and who are born of noble families are worthless if they have no learning. They are just like the *kiṁśuka* blossoms (flowers of the *palāśa* tree) which, though beautiful, have no fragrance. (CNS: 8.21).

- One destitute of wealth is not destitute, he is indeed rich (if he is learned); but the man devoid of learning is destitute in every way. (CNS: 10.1).

- Those who are destitute of learning, penance, knowledge, good disposition, virtue and benevolence are brutes wandering the earth in the form of men. They are burdensome to the earth. (CNS: 10.7).

- He who possesses intelligence is strong; how can the man that is unintelligent be powerful? The elephant of the forest having lost his senses by intoxication was tricked into a lake by a small rabbit. (cf. *Nīti-Śāstra* called *Pañcatantra* by Viṣṇu Śarmā) (CNS: 10.16).

On Education/Educated/Knowledge/Learning

- Though men are endowed with beauty and youth and born in noble families, yet without education, they are like the *palāśa* flower which is void of sweet fragrance. (CNS: 3.8).

- Religion is preserved by wealth; knowledge by diligent

practice; a king by conciliatory words; and a home by a dutiful housewife. (CNS: 5.9).

- The life of an uneducated man is as useless as the tail of a dog which neither covers its rear end, nor protects it from the bites of insects. (CNS: 7.19)

- Knowledge is lost without putting it into practice; a man is lost due to ignorance; an army is lost without a commander; and a woman is lost without a husband. (CNS: 8.8).

- A man who encounters the following three is unfortunate; the death of his wife in his old age, the entrusting of money into the hands of relatives, and depending upon others for food. (CNS: 8.9).

- We should carefully scrutinise that place upon which we step (having it ascertained to be free from filth and living creatures like insects, etc.); we should drink water which has been filtered (through a clean cloth); we should speak only those words which have the sanction of the *Śāstras*; and do that act which we have carefully considered. (CNS: 10.12).

- He who is engrossed in family life will never acquire knowledge; there can be no mercy in the eater of flesh; the greedy man will not be truthful; and purity will not be found in a hunter woman. (CNS: 11.5).

- It is not strange if a man reviles a thing of which he has no knowledge, just as a wild hunter's wife throws away the pearl that is found in the head of an elephant, and picks up a *gunjā* (a type of seed which poor tribals wear as ornaments). (CNS: 11.8).

- Courtesy should be learned from princes, the art of conversation from *Paṇḍits*, lying should be learned from gamblers and deceitful ways should be learned from women. (CNS: 12.8).

- As the man who digs obtains underground water by use of a shovel, so the student attains the knowledge possessed by his preceptor through his service. (CNS: 13.17).

- For one whose heart melts with compassion for all

creatures; what is the necessity of knowledge, liberation, matted hair on the head, and smearing the body with ashes. (CNS: 15.1).

- The scholar who has acquired knowledge by studying innumerable books without the blessings of a bonafide spiritual master does not shine in an assembly of truly learned men just as an illegitimate child is not honoured in society. (CNS: 17.1).

- Men have eating, sleeping, fearing and mating in common with the lower animals. That in which men excel the beasts is discretionary knowledge; hence, indiscreet men who are without knowledge should be regarded as beasts. (CNS: 17.17).

On Women/Wife

- A wicked wife, a false friend, a saucy servant and living in a house with a serpent in it are nothing but death. (CNS: 1.5).

- A wise man should marry a virgin of a respectable family even if she is deformed. He should not marry one of a corrupt family, through beauty. Marriage in a family of equal status is preferable. (CNS: 1.14).

- Do not put your trust in rivers, men who carry weapons, beasts with claws or horns, women, and members of a royal family. (CNS: 1.15).

- Untruthfulness, rashness, guile, stupidity, avarice, uncleanliness and cruelty are women's seven natural flaws. (CNS: 2.1).

- Give your daughter in marriage to a good family, engage your son in learning, see that your enemy comes to grief, and engage your friends in *dharma.* (CNS: 3.3)

- When one is consumed by the sorrows of life, three things give him relief: offspring, a wife, and the company of the Lord's devotees. (CNS: 4.10)

- She is a true wife who is clean (*śuci*), expert, chaste, pleasing to the husband, and truthful. (CNS: 4.13)

- The king, the scholar, and the ascetic *Yogi* who go

abroad are respected; but the woman who wanders is utterly ruined. (CNS: 6.4)

- One single object (a woman) appears in three different ways: to the man who practices austerity it appears as a corpse, to the sensual it appears as a woman, and to the dogs as a lump of flesh. (CNS: 14.15).

- The heart of a crooked woman is not united; it is divided. While she is talking with one man, she looks lustfully at another and thinks fondly of a third in her heart. (CNS: 16.2). The fool (*mūdha*) who fancies that a charming young lady loves him, becomes her slave and he dances like an *śakuntala* (bird) tied to a string. (CNS: 16.3).

- O lady, why are you gazing downward? Has something of yours fallen on the ground? (She replies) O fool, can you not understand the pearl of my youth has slipped away? (CNS:17.20)

On Sons

- He whose son is obedient to him, whose wife's conduct is in accordance with his wishes, and who is content with his riches, has his heaven here on earth. (CNS: 2.3).

- They alone are sons who are devoted to their father. He is a father who supports his sons. He is a friend in whom we can confide, and she only is a wife in whose company the husband feels contented and peaceful. (CNS: 2.4).

- Wise men should always bring up their sons in various moral ways, for children who have knowledge of *Nīti-Śāstra* and are well-behaved become a glory to their family. (CNS: 2.10).

- Those parents who do not educate their sons are their enemies; for as is a crane among swans, so are ignorant so are ignorant sons in a public assembly. (CNS: 2.11).

- Manytimes a bad habit is developed through overindulgence, and often a good one by chastisement, therefore beat your son as well as your pupil; never indulge them. ('Spare the rod and spoil the child.') (CNS: 2.12).

- As a whole forest becomes fragrant by the existence of

a single tree with sweet-smelling blossoms in it, so a family becomes famous by the birth of a virtuous son. (CNS: 3.14).

- As a single withered tree, if set aflame, causes a whole forest to burn, so does a rascal son destroy a whole family. (CNS: 3.15).

- As night looks delightful when the moon shines, so is a family gladdened by even one learned and virtuous son. (CNS: 3.16).

- What is the use of having many sons if they cause grief and vexation? It is better to have only one son from whom the whole family that can derive support and peacefulness. (CNS: 3.17).

- Fondle a son until he is five years of age, and use the stick for another ten years, but when he has attained his sixteenth year treat him as a friend. (CNS: 3.18).

- A single son endowed with good qualities is far better than a hundred devoid of them. For the moon, though one, dispels the darkness, which the stars, though numerous, can not. (CNS: 4.6).

- A still-born son is superior to a foolish son endowed with a long life. The first causes grief. (CNS: 4.7).

- What good is a cow that neither gives milk nor conceives? Similarly, what is the value of the birth of a son if he becomes neither learned nor a pure devotee of the Lord? (CNS: 4.9).

Some Do's

❖ By offending a kinsman, life is lost; by offending others, wealth is lost; by offending the king, everything is lost; and by offending a scholar one's whole family is ruined. *Chāṇakya Nītiśāstra* (CNS) 10.11.

❖ The student (Brahmacārī) should completely renounce the following eight things -- his lust, anger, greed, desire for sweets, sense of decorating the body, excessive curiosity, excessive sleep, and excessive endeavour for bodily maintenance. (CNS: 11.10).

❖ The cuckoos remain silent for a long time (for several seasons) until they are able to sing sweetly (in the Spring) so as to give joy to all. (CNS: 14.17).

❖ We should secure and keep the following: the blessings of meritorious deeds, wealth, grain, the words of the spiritual master, and rare medicines. Otherwise, life becomes impossible. (CNS: 14.18).

❖ Eschew wicked company and associate with saintly persons. Acquire virtue day and night, and always meditate on that which is eternal forgetting that which is temporary. (CNS: 14.19).

Some Don'ts

❖ Do not inhabit a country where you are not respected, or cannot earn your livelihood, have any friends, or cannot acquire knowledge. (CNS: 1.8).

❖ Wise men should never go into a country where there are no means of earning one's livelihood, where the people have no dread of anybody, have no sense of shame, no intelligence, or a charitable disposition. (CNS: 1.10).

❖ Do not keep company with a fool, as we can see him as a two-legged beast. Like an unseen thorn, he pierces the heart with his sharp words. (CNS: 3.7)

❖ Do not pass between two scholars, between a scholar and fire of *Yajña*, between a wife and her husband, a master and his servant, and a plough and an ox. (CNS: 7.5).

❖ Do not let your foot touch fire, the spiritual master or a scholar; it must never touch a cow, a virgin, an old person or a child. (CNS: 7.6).

❖ Do not be very upright in your dealings for you would see by going to the forest that straight trees are cut down while crooked ones are left standing (CNS: 7.12).

❖ The wise man should not be anxious about his food; he should be anxious to be engaged only in *dharma*, the food of each man is created for Him at his birth. (CNS: 12.20).

Code of conduct, in general

❖ Test a servant while in the discharge of his duty, a relative in difficulty, a friend in adversity, and a wife in misfortune. (CNS: 11.1).

❖ He is a **true friend** who does not forsake us in time of need, misfortune, famine, or war, in a king's court, or at the crematorium (*śmaśāna*). (CNS: 1.12).

❖ Even from poison nectar can be extracted, wash and take back gold if it has fallen in filth, receive the highest knowledge from a born person of *Śudra* personality type; so also a girl possessing virtuous qualities (*stri-ratna*) even if she is born in a disreputable family. (CNS: 1.16).

❖ Avoid him who talks sweetly before you but tries to ruin you behind your back, for he is like a pitcher of poison with milk on top. (CNS: 2.5).

❖ Do not put your trust in a bad companion nor even trust an ordinary friend, for if he should get angry with you, he may bring all your secrets to light. (CNS: 2.6)

❖ Do not reveal what you have thought upon doing, but by wise council keep it secret being determined to carry it into execution. (CNS: 2.7).

❖ There does not exist a ruby in every mountain, nor a pearl in the head of every elephant; neither are the *sadhus* to be found everywhere, nor sandal trees in every forest. (CNS: 2.9).

❖ Separation from the wife, disgrace from one's own people, an enemy saved in battle, service to a wicked king, poverty, and a mismanaged assembly: these six kinds of evils, if afflicting a person, *burn him even without fire.* (CNS: 2.14).

❖ He who befriends a man whose conduct is vicious, whose vision impure, and who is notoriously crooked, is rapidly ruined. (CNS: 2.19).

❖ A friendship between equals flourishes, service under a king is respectable, it is good to be business-minded in public dealings, and a beautiful lady is not safe in her own home. (CNS: 2.20).

❖ In this world, whose family is there without blemish? Who is free from sickness and grief? Who is forever happy? (CNS: 3.1).

❖ A man's descent may be discerned by his conduct, his country by his pronunciation of language, his friendship by his warmth and glow, and his capacity to eat by his body. (CNS: 3.2).

❖ What is too heavy for the strong and what place is too distant for those who put forth effort? What country is foreign to a man of true learning? Who can be inimical to one who speaks pleasingly? (CNS: 3.13).

❖ Residing in a small village devoid of proper living facilities, serving a person born of a low mentality and calibre, unwholesome food, a frowning wife, a foolish son, and a widowed daughter burn the body without fire. (CNS: 4.8).

❖ The house of a childless person is a void, all directions are void to one who has no relatives, the heart of a fool is also void, but to a poverty-stricken man all is void. (CNS: 4.14).

❖ Scriptural lessons not put into practice are poison; a meal is poison to him who suffers from indigestion; a social gathering is poison to a poverty-stricken person; and a young wife is poison to an *aged man.* (CNS: 4.15).

❖ That man who is without moral, ethical values and mercy should be rejected. A guru without spiritual knowledge should be rejected. A spouse with an offensive attitude should be given up, and so should relatives who are without affection. (CNS: 4.16).

❖ Constant travel brings old age upon a man; a horse becomes old by being constantly tied up; lack of sexual contact with her husband brings old age upon a woman; and garments become old through being left in the sun. (CNS: 4.17).

❖ Consider again and again the following: the right time, the right friends, the right place, the right means of income, the right ways of spending, and from whom you derive your power. (CNS: 4.18).

❖ Teacher worshipable persons for the students; a person of Brāhmaṇa personality type is worshipable for the persons of Kṣatriya, Vaiśya and Śudra personality types; the husband for the wife; and the guest who comes for food at the midday meal for all. (CNS: 5.1).

❖ As gold is tested in four ways by rubbing, cutting, heating and beating -- so a man should be tested by these four things: his renunciation, his conduct, his qualities and his actions. (CNS: 5.2).

❖ A thing may be dreaded as long as it has not overtaken you, but once it has come upon you, try to get rid of it without hesitation. (CNS: 5.3).

❖ He whose hands are clean does not like to hold an office; he who desires nothing cares not for bodily decorations; he who is only partially educated cannot speak agreeably; and he who speaks out plainly cannot be a deceiver. (CNS: 5.5).

❖ Charity puts an end to poverty; righteous conduct to misery; discretion to ignorance; and scurtiny to fear. (CNS: 5.11).

❖ There is no disease (so destructive) as lust; no enemy like infatuation; no fire like wrath; and no happiness like spiritual knowledge. (CNS: 5.12).

❖ The rain which falls upon the sea is useless; so is food for one who is satiated; in vain is a gift for one who is wealthy; and a burning lamp during the daytime is useless. (CNS: 5.16).

❖ Among birds the crow is vile; among beasts the dog; the ascetic whose sin is abominable, but he who blasphemes others is the worst *chandala*. (CNS: 6.2).

❖ Time perfects all living beings as well as kills them; it alone is awake when all others are asleep. Time is insurmountable. (CNS: 6.7).

❖ A man who encounters the following three is

unfortunate; the death of his wife in his old age, the entrusting of money into the hands of relatives, and depending upon others for food. (CNS: 8.9).

❖ He who neither rouses fear by his anger, nor confers a favour when he is pleased can neither control nor protect. What can he do? (CNS: 9.9).

❖ The serpent may, without being poisonous, raise high its hood, but the show of terror is enough to frighten people -- whether he be venomous or not. (CNS: 9.10).

❖ Generosity, pleasing address, courage and propriety of conduct are not acquired, but are inbred qualities. (CNS: 11.1).

❖ The elephant has a huge body but is controlled by the aṅkuśa (goad): yet, is the goad as large as the elephant? A lighted candle banishes darkness: is the candle as vast as the darkness. A mountain is broken even by a thunderbolt: is the thunderbolt therefore as big as the mountain? No, he whose power prevails is really mighty; what is there in bulk? (CNS: 11.3).

❖ The man who remains a fool even in advanced age is really a fool, just as the Indrāvaruṇa fruit does not become sweet no matter how ripe it might become. (CNS: 12.23).

❖ There are three gems upon this earth; food, water, and pleasing words -- fools (*mūḍhas*) consider pieces of rocks as gems. (CNS: 13.21).

❖ Poverty, disease, sorrow, imprisonment and other evils are the fruits borne by the tree of one's own sins. (CNS: 14.1).

❖ Wealth, a friend, a wife, and a kingdom may be regained; but this body when lost may never be acquired again. (CNS: 14.2).

❖ If men should always retain the state of mind they experience when hearing religious instruction, when present at a crematorium ground, and when in sickness -- then who could not attain liberation. (CNS: 14.5).

❖ If a man should feel before, as he feels after,

repentance -- then who would not attain perfection? (CNS: 14.6).

❖ We should always speak what would please the man of whom we expect a favour, like the hunter who sings sweetly when he desires to shoot a deer. (CNS: 14.9).

❖ He is a pandit (man of knowledge) who speaks what is suitable to the occasion, who renders loving service according to his ability, and who knows the limits of his anger. (CNS: 14.14)

❖ A bad action committed by a great man is not censured (as there is none that can reproach him), and a good action performed by a man of low profile comes to be condemned (because none respects him). Just see: the drinking of nectar is excellent, but it became the cause of Rahu's demise; and the drinking of poison is harmful, but when Lord Shiva (who is exalted) drank it, it became an ornament to his neck (*nila-kaṇṭ ha*). (CNS: 15.7).

❖ A true meal is that which consists of the remnants of a scholar's meal. Love which is shown to others is true love, not that which is cherished for one's own self. To abstain from sin is true wisdom. That is an act of charity which is performed without ostentation. (CNS: 15.8).

❖ For want of discernment, the most precious jewels lie in the dust at the feet of men while bits of glass are worn on their heads. But we should not imagine that the gems have sunk in value, and the bits of glass have risen in importance. **When a person of critical judgement shall appear, each will be given its right position.** (CNS: 15.9).

❖ There are many ways of binding by which one can be dominated and controlled in this world, but the bond of affection is the strongest. For example, take the case of the humble black bee which, although expert at piercing hardened wood, becomes caught in the embrace of its beloved flowers (as the petals close at dusk). (CNS: 15.17).

❖ Although sandalwood, when cut, does not forsake its natural quality of fragrance; so also the elephant does not give up sportiveness though he should grow old. The sugarcane does not cease to be sweet though squeezed in a mill; **so the man of noble extraction does not lose his lofty qualities, no matter how pinched he is by poverty.** (CNS: 15.18).

❖ A man attains greatness by his merits, not simply by occupying an exalted seat. Can we call a crow an eagle (garuda) simply because he sits on the top of a tall building. (CNS: 16.6).

❖ The man who is praised by others as great is regarded as worthy, though he may be really void of all merit. But **the man who sings his own praises lowers himself in the estimation of others though he should be Indra** (the possessor of all excellences). (CNS: 16.8).

❖ If good qualities should characterise a man of discrimination, the brilliance of his qualities will be recognised just as a gem which is essentially bright really shines when fixed in an ornament of gold. (CNS: 16.9).

❖ Even one who by his qualities appears to be all-knowing suffers without patronage; the gem, though precious, requires a gold setting. (CNS:16.10).

❖ All charities and sacrifices (performed for fruitful gain) bring only temporary results, but gifts made to deserving persons and protection offered to all creatures shall never perish. (CNS: 16.14).

❖ It is better to die than to preserve this life by incurring disgrace. The loss of life causes but a moment's grief, but disgrace brings grief every day to one's life. (CNS: 16.16).

❖ All the creatures are pleased by loving words; and therefore we should address words that are pleasing to all, for there is no lack of sweet words. (CNS: 16.17).

❖ O *Ketki* flower! Serpents live in your midst, you bear no edible fruits, your leaves are covered with thorns, you are crooked in growth, you thrive in mud, and you are not easily accessible. Still, for your exceptional fragrance, you are as dear as a kinsmen to others. Hence, a single excellence overcomes a multitude of blemishes. (CNS:17.21).

Dependance

❖ Foolishness is indeed painful, and verily so is youth, but more painful by far than either is being obliged in another person's house. (CNS: 2.8).

❖ There is no water like rainwater; **no strength like one's own**; no light like that of the eyes; and no wealth more dear than food grain. (CNS: 5.17).

❖ It is better to live under a tree in a jungle inhabited by tigers and elephants, to maintain oneself in such a place with ripe fruits and spring water, to lie down on grass and to wear the ragged barks of trees than to live amongst one's relations when reduced to poverty. (CNS: 10.12).

❖ The moon, who is the abode of nectar and the presiding deity of all medicines, although immortal like amṛta and resplendent in form, loses the brilliance of his rays when he repairs to the abode of the sun (day time). Therefore, will not an ordinary man be made to feel inferior by going to live at the house of another? (CNS: 15.14).

ON KINGS

- Trees on a riverbank, a woman in another man's house, and kings without counsellors go without doubt to swift destruction. (CNS: 2.15).

- A scholar's strength is in his learning, a king's strength is in his army, a businessman's strength is in his wealth and a worker's strength is in his attitude of service. (CNS: 2.16).

- The prostitute has to forsake a man who has no money, the subject a king that cannot defend him, the birds a tree that bears no fruit, and the guests a house after they have finished their meals. (CNS: 2.17).

- Of a rascal and a serpent, the serpent is the better of the two, for he strikes only at the time he is destined to kill, while the former at every step. (CNS: 3.5).

- Therefore, kings gather round themselves men of good families, for they never forsake them either at the beginning, the middle or the end. (CNS: 3.4).

- Kings speak for once, men of learning once, and the daughter is given in marriage once. All these things happen once and only once. (CNS: 4.11).

- The king is responsible for the sins committed by his subjects; the counselor for those of the king; a husband for those of his wife; and the guru for those of his pupils. (CNS: 6.10).

- It is better to be without a kingdom than to rule over a petty one; better to be without a friend than to befriend a rascal; better to be without a disciple than to have a stupid one; and better to be without a wife than to have a bad one. (CNS: 6.13).

- How can people be made happy in a petty kingdom? What peace can we expect from a rascal friend? What happiness can we have at home in the company of a bad wife? How can renown be gained by instructing an unworthy disciple? (CNS: 6.14).

- The power of a king lies in his mighty arms; that of a scholar in his knowledge; and that of a woman in her beauty youth and sweet words. (CNS: 7.11).

- He who forsakes his own community and joins another perishes as the king who embraces an unrighteous path. (CNS: 11.2).

- If the king is virtuous, then the subjects are also virtuous. If the king is sinful, then the subjects also become sinful. If he is mediocre, then the subjects are mediocre. The subjects follow the example of the king. In short, as is the king so are the subjects. (CNS: 13.8).

- It is ruinous to be familiar with the king, fire, the religious preceptor, and a woman. To be altogether indifferent of them is to be deprived of the opportunity to benefit ourselves, hence our association with them must be from a safe distance. (CNS: 14.10).

• We should always deal cautiously with fire, water, women, foolish people, serpents, and members of a royal family; for they may, when the occasion presents itself, at once bring about our death. (CNS: 14.11).

• A king, a prostitute, Lord Yamaraja, fire, a thief, a young boy, and a beggar cannot understand the suffering of others. The eighth of this category is the tax collector. (CNS: 17.19).

ON PROVIDENCE/FATE

• These five: the life-span, the type of work, wealth, learning and the time of one's death are determined while one is in the womb. (CNS: 4.1)

• Though persons are born from the same womb and under the same stars, they do not become alike in disposition as the thousand fruits of the badari tree. (CNS: 5.4).

• As is the desire of Providence, so functions one's intellect; one's activities are also controlled by Providence; and by the will of Providence one is surrounded by helpers. (CNS: 6.6).

• Perhaps nobody has advised Lord Brahma, the creator, to impart perfume to gold; fruit to the sugarcane; flowers to the sandalwood tree; wealth to the learned; and long life to the king. (CNS: 9.3).

• Fate makes a beggar a king and a king a beggar. He makes a rich man poor and a poor man rich. (CNS: 10.5).

• What fault of spring that the bamboo shoot has no leaves? What fault of the Sun if the owl cannot see during the daytime? Is it the fault of the clouds if no raindrops fall into the mouth of the Chātaka bird? Who can erase what Lord Brahmā has inscribed upon our foreheads at the time of birth? (CNS: 12.6).

• We should not fret for what is past, nor should we be anxious about the future; men of discernment deal only with the present moment. (CNS: 13.2).

- Even as the unborn baby is in the womb of his mother, these five are fixed as his life destiny: his life span, his activities, his acquisition of wealth and knowledge, and his time of death. (CNS: 13.4).

Father/ Mother

- These five are your father; he who gave you birth, girdled you with the sacred thread, teaches you, provides you with food, and protects you from fearful situations. (CNS: 5.22).

- These five should be considered as mother; the king's wife, the preceptor's wife, the friend's wife, your wife's mother, and your own mother. (CNS: 5.23).

- A father who is a chronic debtor, an adulterous mother, a beautiful wife, and an unlearned son are enemies (in one's own home). (CNS: 6.11).

Conciliation

➢ Conciliate a covetous man by means of a gift, an obstinate man with folded hands in salutation, a fool by humouring him, and a learned man by truthful words. (CNS: 6.12)

➢ Conciliate a strong man by submission, a wicked man by opposition, and the one whose power is equal to yours by politeness or force. (CNS: 7.10).

➢ There is no treasure on earth the gift of which will cancel the debt a disciple owes his guru for having taught him even a single letter. (CNS: 15.2).

Learn from these twenty

➢ Learn one thing from a lion; one from a crane; four from a cock; five from a crow; six from a dog; and three from an donkey. (CNS: 6.15).

➢ The one excellent thing that can be learned from a lion is that whatever a man intends doing should be done by him with a whole-hearted and strenuous effort. (CNS: 6.16).

➢ The wise man should restrain his senses like the crane and accomplish his purpose with due knowledge of his place, time and ability. (CNS: 6.17).

➢ To wake at the proper time; to take a bold stand and fight; to make a fair division (of property) among relations; and to earn one's own bread by personal exertion are the four excellent things to be learned from a cock. (CNS: 6.18).

➢ Union in privacy (with one's wife); boldness; storing away useful items; watchfulness; and not easily trusting others; these five things are to be learned from a crow. (CNS: 6.19).

➢ Contentment with little or nothing to eat although one may have a great appetite; to awaken instantly although one may be in a deep slumber; unflinching devotion to the master; and bravery; these six qualities should be learned from the dog. (CNS:6.20).

➢ Although an donkey is tired, he continues to carry his burden; he is unmindful of cold and heat; and he is always contented; these three things should be learned from the ass (CNS: 6.21).

➢ He who shall practice these twenty virtues shall become invincible in all his undertakings. (CNS: 6.22).

Should not reveal

➢ A wise man should not reveal his loss of wealth, the vexation of his mind, the misconduct of his own wife, base words spoken by others, and disgrace that has befallen him. (CNS: 7.1).

➢ A wise man should not divulge the formula of a medicine which he has well prepared; an act of charity which he has performed; domestic conflicts; private affairs with his wife; poorly prepared food he may have been offered; or slang he may have heard. (CNS: 14.16.).

Happiness

➢ He who gives up shyness in monetary dealings, in

acquiring knowledge, in eating and in business, becomes happy. (CNS: 7.2).

➢ The happiness and peace attained by those satisfied by the nectar of spiritual tranquillity is not attained by greedy persons restlessly moving here and there. (CNS: 12:2)

➢ Those men are happy in this world, who are generous towards their relatives, kind to strangers, indifferent to the wicked, loving to the good, shrewd in their dealings with the base, frank with the learned, courageous with enemies, humble with elders and stern with the wife. (CNS: 12.3).

➢ He whose actions are disorganised has no happiness either in the midst of men or in a jungle -- in the midst of men his heart burns by social contacts, and his helplessness burns him in the forest. (CNS: 13.16).

Satisfied/Not Satisfied

➢ One should feel satisfied with the following three things; his own wife, food given by Providence and wealth acquired by honest effort; but one should never feel satisfied with the following three; study, chanting the holy names of the God (japa) and charity. (CNS: 7.4).

➢ Scholars find satisfaction in a good meal, peacocks in the peal of thunder, a sadhu in seeing the prosperity of others, and the wicked in the misery of others. (CNS: 7.9).

Wicked person

➢ Keep one thousand cubits away from an elephant, a hundred from a horse, ten from a horned beast, but keep away from the wicked by leaving the country. (CNS:7.7).

➢ An elephant is controlled by a goad (*Aṅkuśa*), a horse by a slap of the hand, a horned animal with the show of a stick, and a rascal with a sword. (CNS: 7.8).

➢ Those base men who speak of the secret faults of others destroy themselves like serpents who stray onto anthills. (CNS: 9.2).

➢ Those that are empty-minded cannot be benefited from

instruction. Bamboo does not acquire the quality of sandalwood by being associated with the Malaya Mountain. (CNS: 10.8).

➢ Nothing can reform a bad man, just as the posterios cannot become a superior part of the body though washed one hundred times. (CNS: 10.10).

➢ The wicked man will not attain sanctity even if he is instructed in different ways, and the Neem tree will not become sweet even if it is sprinkled from the top to the roots with milk and ghee. (CNS: 11.6).

➢ A wicked man may develop saintly qualities in the company of a devotee, but a devotee does not become impious in the company of a wicked person. The earth is scented by a flower that falls upon it, but the flower does not contact the odour of the earth. (CNS: 12.7).

➢ The hearts of base men burn before the fire of other's fame, and they slander them being themselves unable to rise to such a high position. (CNS: 13.11).

➢ There are two ways to get rid of thorns and wicked persons; using footwear in the first case and in the second shaming them so that they cannot raise their faces again thus keeping them at a distance. (CNS: 15.3).

➢ Who is there who, having become rich, has not become proud? What licentious man has put an end to his calamities? What man in this world has not been overcome by a woman? Who is always loved by the king? Who is there who has not been overcome by the ravages of time? What beggar has attained glory? Who has become happy by contracting the vices of the wicked? (CNS: 16.4).

➢ We should repay the favours of others by acts of kindness; so also should we return evil for evil in which there is no sin, for it is necessary to pay a wicked man in his own coin. (CNS: 17.2).

➢ There is poison in the fang of the serpent, in the mouth of the fly and in the sting of a scorpion; but the wicked man is saturated with it. (CNS: 17.8).

Dietary code of conduct

- The lamp eats up the darkness and therefore it makes the lamp black; in the same way, according to the nature of our diet (*Sattva*, *Rajas*, or *Tamas*) we produce offspring in similar quality. (CNS: 8.3).

- The wise who discern the essence of things have declared that the yavana (meat-eater) is equal in baseness to a thousand of *Chāṇḍalas*), and hence a yavana is the basest of men; indeed there is no one more base. (CNS: 8.5).

- Water is the medicine for indigestion; it is invigorating when the food that is eaten is well digested; it is like nectar when taken in the middle of the food. (CNS: 8.7).

- The earth is encumbered with the weight of the flesh-eaters, wine-bibblers, dolts and blockheads, who are beasts in the form of men. (CNS: 8.22).

- Nectar (*amṛta*) is the best among medicines; eating good food is the best of all types of material happiness; the eye is the chief among all organs; and the head occupies the chief position among all parts of the body. (CNS: 9.4).

- Poverty is set off by fortitude; shabby garments by keeping them clean; bad food by warming it; and ugliness by good behaviour. (CNS: 9.14).

- He who for one year eats his meals silently (inwardly meditating upon God's prasādam); attains emanicipation for a thousand crores of years. (Note: one crore equals ten million) (CNS: 11.9).

Purity

- The purity of speech, of the mind, of the senses, and of a compassionate heart are needed by one who desires to rise to the divine platform. (CNS: 7.20)

- After having rubbed oil on the body, after encountering the smoke from a funeral pyre, after sexual intercourse, and after being shaved, one remains impure until he bathes. (CNS: 8.6).

- Water seeping into the earth is pure; and a devoted wife is pure; the king who is the benefactor of his people is pure; and pure is the scholar who is contented with what he has. (CNS: 8.17).

- Discontented scholars, contented kings, shy prostitutes, and immodest housewives are ruined. (CNS: 8.18).

- Mental dirt cannot be washed away even by one-hundred baths in the sacred waters, just as a wine pot cannot be purified even by evaporating all the wine by fire. (CNS: 11.7).

- He who wears unclean garments, has dirty teeth, is a glutton, speaks unkindly and sleeps after sunrise -- although he may be the greatest personality -- will lose the favour of Lakshmi. (CNS: 15.4).

Contentment

- There is no austerity equal to a balanced mind, and there is no happiness equal to contentment; there is no disease like covetousness and no virtue like mercy. (CNS: 8.13).

- Anger is a personification of Yama (the demigod of death); thirst is like the hellish river Vaitarani; knowledge is like a Kāmadhenu (the cow of plenty); and contentment is like Nandanavana. (CNS: 8.14).

- Who realises all the happiness he desires everything is in the hands of God. Therefore one should learn contentment. (CNS: 13.14).

Ornament

- Moral excellence is an ornament for personal beauty; righteous conduct, for high birth; success for learning; and proper spending for wealth. (CNS: 8.15).

- The hand is not so well adorned by ornaments as by charitable offerings; one does not become clean by smearing sandalwood paste upon the body as by taking a bath; one does not become so much satisfied by dinner as by having respect shown to him; and salvation is not attained by self-adornment as by cultivation of spiritual knowledge. (CNS: 17.12).

Spoiled/ ruined

- The king, the scholar, and the ascetic yogi who go abroad are respected; but the woman who wanders is utterly ruined. (CNS: 6.4)

- Beauty is spoiled by an immoral nature; noble birth by bad conduct; learning, without being perfected; and wealth by not being properly utilised. (CNS: 8.16).

- The unthinking spender, the homeless urchin, the quarrel monger, the man who neglects his wife and is heedless in his actions -- all these will soon come to ruination. (CNS: 12.19).

- He who is prepared for the future and he who deals cleverly with any situation that may arise are both happy; but the fatalistic man who wholly depends on luck is ruined. (CNS: 13.7).

- Indolent application ruins study; money is lost when entrusted to others; a farmer who sows his seeds sparsely is ruined; and an army is lost for want of a commander. (CNS: 5.7).

Seven ought to be awakened/not awakened

➢ The student, the servant, the traveller, the hungry person, the frightened man, the treasury guard, and the steward: these seven ought to be awakened if they fall asleep. (CNS: 9.6)

➢ The serpent, the king, the tiger, the stinging wasp, the small child, the dog owned by other people, and the fool: these seven ought not to be awakened from sleep. (CNS: 9.7).

Enemy

- The beggar is a miser's enemy; the wise counsellor is the fool's enemy; the husband is an adulterous wife's enemy; and the Moon is the enemy of the thief. (CNS: 10.6).

- The enemy can be overcome by the union of large numbers, just as grass through its collectiveness wards off erosion caused by heavy rainfall. (CNS: 14.3).

Qualities of a Brāhmaṇa personality type

➢ He alone has a true Brāhmaṇa personality who is satisfied with one meal a day, who has the six *saṁskāras* (or acts of purification such as *garbhādhāna*, etc.) performed for him, and who cohabits with his wife only once in a month on an auspicious day after her menses. (CNS: 10.12).

➢ The Brāhmaṇa is like a tree; his prayers are the roots, his chanting of the Vedas are the branches, and his religious acts are the leaves. Consequently, effort should be made to preserve his roots for if the roots are destroyed there can be no branches or leaves. (CNS: 10.13).

➢ If a person of a profession of Brāhmaṇa becomes engrossed in worldly affairs, brings up cows and is engaged in trade, he is called as Vaiśya. (CNS: 11.13).

➢ If a person of a profession of Brāhmaṇa deals in lac-die, articles, oil, indigo, silken cloth, honey, clarified butter, liquor, and flesh, he will be called as a Śudra. (CNS: 11.14).

➢ If a person of a profession of Brāhmaṇa thwarts the doings of others, is hypocritical, selfish, and a deceitful hater, and while speaking mildly cherishes cruelty in his heart, he will be called a cat. (CNS: 11.15).

➢ If a person of a profession of Brāhmaṇa destroys a pond, a well, a tank, a garden or a temple will be called a mleccha. (CNS: 11.16).

➢ If a person of a profession of Brāhmaṇa steals the property of the Deities and the spiritual preceptor, who cohabits with another's wife, and who maintains himself by eating anything and everything, he will be called a Chāṇḍāla. (CNS: 11.17).

➢ One who devotedly gives a little to a person of Brāhmaṇa profession and personality who is in distress is recompensed abundantly. Hence, O Prince, what is given to a good Brāhmaṇa is got back not in an equal quantity, but in an infinitely higher degree. (CNS: 12.2).

➢ Those blessed souls are certainly elevated who, while

crossing the ocean of life, take shelter of a genuine Brāhmaṇa, who is likened unto a boat. They are unlike passengers aboard an ordinary ship which runs the risk of sinking. (CNS: 15.3).

Quality of a Gṛhastha (householder)

• He is a blessed gṛhasta (householder) in whose house there is a blissful atmosphere, whose sons are talented, whose wife speaks sweetly, whose wealth is enough to satisfy his desires, who finds pleasure in the company of his wife, whose servants are obedient, in whose house hospitality is shown, the auspicious Supreme Lord is worshiped daily, delicious food and drink is partaken, and who finds joy in the company of devotees. (CNS: 12.1).

• The house in which the lotus feet of scholars are not washed, in which Vedic mantras are not loudly recited, and in which the holy rites of *Svāha* (Yajña) and Svadhā (offerings to the creatures around) are not performed, is like a crematorium. (CNS: 12.10).

• He who is overly attached to his family members experiences fear and sorrow, for the root of all grief is attachment. Thus one should discard attachment to be happy. (CNS: 13.6).

• He is a Cāṇḍāla who eats his dinner without entertaining the stranger who has come to his house quite accidentally, having travelled from a long distance and is wearied. (CNS: 15.11).

• What is there to be enjoyed in the world of Lord Indra for one whose wife is loving and virtuous, who possesses wealth, who has a well-behaved son endowed with good qualities, and who has grandchildren born of his children? (CNS: 17.16).

Polluted

• O jackal, leave aside the body of that man at once, whose hands have never given in charity, whose ears have not heard the voice of learning, whose eyes have not beheld a pure devotee of the Lord, whose feet have never traversed to holy places, whose belly is filled with things obtained by crooked practices, and whose head is held high in vanity. Do not eat it, O jackal, otherwise, you will become polluted. (CNS: 12.4).

Friend

➢ Knowledge is a friend on the journey; a wife in the house; medicine in sickness; and ethical and moral values are the only friend after death. (CNS: 5.15).

➢ Realised knowledge (*vidyā*) is our friend while travelling, the wife is a friend at home, medicine is the friend of a sick man, and meritorious deeds are the friends at death. (CNS: 12.17).

➢ He who has wealth has friends and relations; he alone survives and is respected as a man. (CNS: 7.15)

Spread out

➢ Oil on water, a secret communicated to a base man, a gift given to a worthy receiver, and scriptural instruction given to an intelligent man spread out by virtue of their nature. (CNS: 14.4)

➢ A servant is tested while in the discharge of his duty, a relative in difficulty, a friend in adversity, and a wife is tested in misfortune.

➢ There is poison in the fang of the serpent, in the mouth of the fly and in the sting of a scorpion; but the wicked man is saturated with it.

➢ Do not be very upright in your dealings for you would see by going to the forest that straight trees are cut down while crooked ones are left standing.'

➢ A person should not be too honest. Straight trees are cut first and honest people are screwed first.' 'Even if a snake is not poisonous, it should pretend to be venomous.' 'The biggest guru-mantra is: Never share your secrets with anybody. It will destroy you.

➢ Before you start some work, always ask yourself three questions - Why am I doing it, What the results might be and whether I Will be successful. Only when you think deeply and find satisfactory answers to these questions, go ahead.

➢ As soon as the fear approaches near, attack and destroy it. The world's biggest power is the youth and beauty of a woman.

➢ Once you start working on something, don't be afraid of failure and don't abandon it. People who work sincerely are the happiest.

➢ The fragrance of flowers spreads only in the direction of the wind. But the goodness of a person spreads in all directions. A man is great by deeds, not by birth. Never make friends with people who are above or below you in status. Such friendships will never give you any happiness.

➢ Treat your kids like a darling for the first five years. For the next five years, scold them. By the time they turn sixteen, treat them like a friend. Your grown-up children are your best friends.

➢ Books are as useful to a stupid person as a mirror is useful to a blind person. Education is the best friend. An educated person is respected everywhere. Education beats the beauty and the youth.

➢ The serpent, the king, the tiger, the stinging wasp, the small child, the dog owned by other people, and the fool: these seven ought not to be awakened from sleep.

➢ He who lives in our heart is near though he may actually be far away; but he who is not in our heart is far though he may really be nearby.

➢ Let not a single day pass without your learning a verse, half a verse, or a quarter part of it, or even one letter of it; nor without attending to charity, study and other pious activity.

➢ One whose knowledge is confined to books and whose wealth is in the possession of others, can use neither his knowledge nor wealth when the need for them arises.

➢ He who is overly attached to his family members

experiences fear and sorrow, for the root of all grief is attachment. Thus one should discard attachment to be happy.

➢ The fragrance of flowers spreads only in the direction of the wind. But the goodness of a person spreads in all directions.

➢ The world's biggest power is the youth and beauty of a woman.

➢ The life of an uneducated man is as useless as the tail of a dog which neither covers its rear end, not protects it from the bites of insects.

➢ A man is born alone and dies alone; and he experiences the good and bad consequences of his karma alone; and he goes alone to hell or the Supreme abode.

➢ It is better to die than to preserve this life by incurring disgrace. The loss of life causes but a moment's grief, but disgrace brings grief every day of one's life.

➢ There is some self-interest behind every friendship. There is no friendship without self-interests. This is a bitter truth. Never make friends with people who are above or below you in status. Such friends will never give you any happiness.

Reference

1. *Chāṇakya Nīti Śāstra*: The Political Ethics of Chāṇakya Paṇḍit : Miles Davis (Patita Pavana dasa), ISCKON (1981).
2. Sri K. Raghunathaji's version of '*Vṛddha-Chāṇakya - The Maxims of Chāṇakya*' (Family Printing Press, Bombay, 1890).

www.ingramcontent.com/pod-product-compliance
Lightning Source LLC
Chambersburg PA
CBHW032121040426
42449CB00005B/209
* 9 7 8 8 1 8 7 7 1 0 9 4 3 *